A DIFFERENT PERSPECTIVE ON
HOW TO REACH
HEAVEN

YOU MUST BE BORN AGAIN

LeeRoy U. Bailey, Jr.

"... ON EITHER SIDE OF THE RIVER, WAS
THERE THE TREE OF LIFE..."
REVELATION 22:2

ISBN 978-1-965679-98-2 (Paperback)
ISBN 978-1-965679-99-9 (Ebook)

Scriptures in quotations that are not
specified are taken from the Holy Bible,
King James Version, Cambridge, 1769.
Used by permission. All rights reserved.

Scripture quotations marked "NKJV" are
taken from The New King James Version/
Thomas Nelson Publishers, Nashville:
Thomas Nelson Publishers. Copyright © 1982
Used by permission. All rights reserved.

Scripture quotations marked "TEV" are taken from
The Good News Bible: Today's English Version,
New York: American Bible Society, Copyright ©
1992. Used by permission. All rights reserved.

Inquiries and Book Orders should be addressed to:

Leavitt Peak Press
17901 Pioneer Blvd Ste L #298,
Artesia, California 90701
Phone #: 2092191548

To saints, sinners,
winners, losers, and the church

"For out of much affliction and anguish of heart
I wrote unto you with many tears; not that ye
should be grieved, but that ye might know the love
which I have more abundantly unto you"
(2nd Corinthians 2:4).

Endorsement

"This book is a great read, LeeRoy Bailey is a dynamic writer. This book speaks for itself and needs no introduction. LeeRoy was truly inspired by the Holy Ghost as he wrote this masterpiece. He is obedient and is a wonderful student of mine. He latched on to my every word because he knows they are inspired by God. I am very proud of him. This book touched on everything to get you to heaven. It touched on holy living, sins, baptism, speaking with other tongues, being saved, and many other topics in Christ. I can guarantee you that this book is an original, divinely inspired by God. Do not miss out on this life changing experience. You must have it. This book is phenomenal! I am not just saying all this because I am LeeRoy's pastor, but this book is truly a gem."

– Kurt W. Geddis, Pastor

Acknowledgments

Praise the Lord, saints, Alleluia! First of all, I want to give all glory, honor, and praises to my Lord and Savior Jesus Christ who is first in my life. He is my source, my refuge, my rock, my sword, my shield, my comforter, my guide, my wheel in the middle of the wheel, and my everything. There is none other like Him. He sits on High and looks down low. Thank you Jesus for the King James Version of your Word that was mostly used throughout this book, for your many blessings, and all that you have given unto me. Amen! I want to give a special honor to my pastor, Elder Kurt W. Geddis, who with the vision from God made this book a possibility. Pastor, besides Jesus, you are the light that guides me. I humble myself before you. You are a true man of God and I owe you my life. I thank you for allowing Jesus to use you. Everyday, I thank God for you, sir. I want to thank Mother Geddis for being an inspiration and a dynamic example of what a true woman servant of the Lord ought to be. Minister Geddis, thank you for ministering unto us. My church brothers and sisters at large, I love you, your prayers and testimonies were what brought me closer to the Lord and allowed Him to fill me with His precious gift of the Holy Ghost, I truly thank you. Brother Jon Dyer, I thank you for listening to the Lord and allowed Him to use you as a vessel to bring a wretch like me into the church, the apostolic way of wor shipping. Brother, I truly thank you. There are no words in this world that could possibly express my gratitude. All I can humbly say is thank God for you, Brother Dyer.

This book is also inspired by various brothers fellowshipping and talking with me about Jesus. Brothers Gbarwea, Akeyo, Otieno, Powell, Johnson, and Hazard. Thank God for you. Deacon Joseph Black, sir, I thank you for all the time given in helping me to edit this work of the Lord. God surely has many blessings with your name written on them. Sister Kapri Gunn, thank you for being my mini-helper in finding Bible verses, for your prayers, and for your encouraging words as I write early in the morning and late at night. Thank you for being such a kind soul. I love you dearly. I can see the Lord working in you and I know you really love Jesus. God bless you. Antenique Chambers, thank God for you. Whether you stay here in Massachusetts or head back to California, I will always be here for you. In the mighty name of Jesus, I pray that God will keep and guide you in all that you do. May God's blessings be upon you.

I also want to thank my biological father, Leroy Bailey. I truly learned a lot from him. He allowed me to be the man I am today. I never experienced drugs, alcohol, or any other sinful things in his household.

He always taught me to be a righteous man. I thank you, dad. My biological brother, Omar, thank you for encouraging me to press onward. I love you with all my heart. Simone, my dearly beloved biological sister, thank you for taking care of me when I was a youngster growing up. I know that because of you I stayed out of trouble. Patrick Francis, thank you for being there for my sister. My dearly beloved mother, Elaine McEnnis, I love you with everything that is in me. I can never repay you for the nine months of pain you bore with me. No matter what our differences may be, I will forever love you. Mom, I will never forget the Thursday night in April of 2007, you traveled to Massachusetts to visit me, came to church with me the Friday night, got re-baptized in Jesus's name, then received the Holy Ghost during Sunday morning worship: speaking with other tongues as the Spirit gave you utterance, rolling around on the floor, and then went back to New York, Monday afternoon. This was one of the best moments in my life. Thank you, and may God bless you with all that your heart desires.

I also want to thank God again for delivering me from chasing after women and presenting my members unto unrighteousness. A true man of God needs a virtuous woman, a wife who respects and loves the Lord first, and then her husband as she would love herself. I thank you Jesus. I want to also thank Victoria Brooks-McDonald who said to a group of students at Union College, "Look out for LeeRoy, you are going to read about him one day." Noteworthy, special thanks again to Jon Dyer, Antenique Chambers, Pastor Kurt Geddis, and others such as Jessica Rodriguez, Andrea Johnson, Pastor Chambers, and Fr. James Mazzone for their contributions to the writing of this book. Last but not least, I want to thank you for reading this book. I know that the Lord will touch your heart in a mighty way and you will truly be blessed. May God bless you.

CONTENTS

INTRODUCTION

In this book, I will tell how the Lord truly saved a poor sinner like me. First of all, I want you to know that I am no better than you. He did it for me and He will do it for you too. All you have to do is let go, open your heart, and let Him in. Anyhow, let me ask you two dear questions: What if you live for the Lord, get baptized in Jesus's name like Peter said in *Acts* 2:38, get filled with the Holy Ghost, and remain true to the word of God, but then found out Jesus is not real? Well, I think you could just continue living. No harm in that.

But, what if you live a lying, fornicating, stealing, partying, killing, adulterous, prideful, lustful, anyone of the above sinful life, then come to find out that Jesus is real as I know He is and that His every word is true, what will you do then? I do not know about you, but I refuse to find out the hard way. The Bible reads in *Romans 6:23*, " ... the wages of sin is death; but the gift of God is eternal life through Jesus Christ our Lord."

The Lord gave me the vision to write this book. He then confirmed it with my pastor by allowing him to share with me the same vision that he had from the Lord without knowing about my vision. I was on the phone with my pastor one night when he said, "The Lord told me that you will write a book that will be a phenomenon and it will change many lives." He then gave me the title of this book as God gave it to him. Jesus is real! I never shared my vision with my pastor or anyone because I thought nothing of it. God is good. He is so very good. Open your hearts, people, time is at hand, and He is coming real soon.

Friends, it is not about religion. There are so many religions out there: Christianity, Catholicism, Islam, Judaism, Buddhism, and Taoism to name a few. Plus, there are also different sects of religions under each of the very few religions mentioned above. Like I wrote before, it is not about religion, religion is a duty; it is all about the Word, the things Jesus said. Many religions have a form of godliness, but deny the power thereof: *from such turn away* (*2nd Timothy* 3:5). Religions of today that do believe in Jesus deny the power of the Holy Ghost. It is as if the Holy Ghost is quiet, dormant, and cannot speak for Himself. People, be godly, focus on the Word of God, not the religion. You need to know how you can be saved. " ... Except a man be born of water and of the Spirit, he cannot enter into the kingdom of God. That which is born of the flesh is flesh; and that which is born of the Spirit is spirit. Marvel not that I said unto thee, Ye must be born again" (*John* 3:5–7). Not only do you need to be baptized by the water to be saved, you also need to be baptized by the Spirit, which is the Holy Ghost. How does one receive the Holy Ghost? Peter said, " … Repent and be baptized every one of you in the name of Jesus Christ for the remission (pardon) of sins, and ye shall receive the gift of the Holy Ghost" (*Acts* 2:38). Paul, the great apostle then wrote, "Know ye not that so many of us as were baptized into Jesus Christ were baptized into His death" (*Romans* 6:3)? There is no interpretation to be made from these scriptures. God does not need man to interpret His Word. He said what He said, plain and simple. People, what the world needs today and tomorrow, is Jesus. "Who is this Jesus?" some may ask.

Follow me here, the Bible reads in the *Book of John* that the Word is God, He is the Word, and Jesus is the Word. Thus, Jesus is God. "In the beginning was the Word, and the Word was with God, and the Word was God … and the Word was made flesh, and dwelt among us … " (*John* 1:1 *and John* 1:14). That flesh was Jesus Christ Himself. Still do not believe that Jesus is God? Jesus said, "Before Abraham was, I Am" (*John* 8:58). Notice here that Jesus did not say I was. I will repeat, He said, "Before Abraham was, I Am." This statement is not only improper, it is also improper English. However, our standard cannot hold a candlestick to Jesus. There is no other way to say it, because Jesus still is, not a "has been." People, being baptized in the phrase "Father, Son, and Holy Spirit, in Jesus's name" is not the correct way to be baptized. There is only, one baptism, one God, and one Father of us all, who is also in all of us (*Ephesians*

4:5–6). You only need to be baptized in the name of Jesus Christ. There is power in His name. Jesus came to save us from our sins (*Matthew* 1:21). We need to be washed in His precious blood (*Revelation* 7:14).

The water represents His blood and being immersed completely into the water in the name of Jesus symbolizes being washed in the blood of Jesus. This is a necessity to *reach heaven*. Accepting Christ as your Savior and believing in the Immaculate Conception (virgin birth) are key steps to salvation, but, according to the scriptures, these alone will not save you. If you want to see the kingdom of heaven and for your sins to be washed away completely, be baptized and receive the gift of the Holy Ghost the right way. There is only one way. Man is wrong, but the Word of God is right (*Romans* 3:4). May God bless you and have mercy upon your soul.

1

My journey with Jesus

My Life

Oh, how sweet it is resting in the arms of Jesus, walking in the newness of life, being filled with the Holy Ghost that runs so deep within my soul, and speaking with other tongues as the Spirit gives utterance. In *Jeremiah* 20:9, Jeremiah wrote that the Word of God was like a burning *fire* shut up in his bones, which he could not control. I tell you, this is what the Holy Ghost/Spirit feels like. Wildly being shocked all over with electricity pumping through my veins. Oh, what a powerful and glorious feeling! I challenge you to want this power. The Holy Ghost feels so very good. The Spirit of the Lord is like a river coming down and reigning all over the earth. Alleluia!

In this chapter, I want to tell you a little about how I got started. I am a Jamaican-born American citizen. I was born on February 6th, 1981 in Spanish Town, St. Catherine. Since I came to know myself, my family and I were always in church. We were in church everyday because of my grandmother, Mrs. Gladys McEnnis. Church to me back then was so very boring. Then again I was a young child, what did I know? I always liked the worshipping part of the service, it just felt right. However, when the preacher started preaching, I started sleeping. I just could not fathom the concept of going to church everyday. Nevertheless, my grandmother knew all along why we needed to go to church. I thank her dearly for bringing me into the church as a young child. Children surely will live what they learn! Church and Jesus have been rooted in me.

All the same, I lived with my mother, her parents, and my sister. My entire extended family was always around also. There were my uncles, aunts, and cousins. We all lived in one big yard with different houses attached together. Our neighborhood was one of abject poverty, leading much of the youth to a life of crime, mostly against one another. As a result of such cruelty against each other, rival gangs sprung up all over our neighborhood. Gangs are all over the world, right? But, not like these gangs in Jamaica. These thugs would kill anything that breathes. One head gang member went to the house of one of his rivals and found the young man and his sister there. He raped the young man's sister as the young man watched helplessly. He then forced the young man to rape his own sister.

Did all this suffice his anger? He then burned the house to the ground. I am not sure if the young man and his sister were left to be burned with the house, but I would surely assume so. That was the point of him going to his rival's home in the first place. He wanted to humiliate and kill him. How can one live after raping one's own sister? If he was not dead physically, he was certainly dead mentally. Who could it be leading these individuals astray but the devil and his many legions. This brute had no heart. He killed many people and animals. He did not care who you were, big, small, pregnant, short, or tall. He would shoot to kill you as well. If you owned a store or business, you had to pay him a portion of your earnings or it is "out of business" for you. People in the community had to pay him "tithes." This man was playing God. Thus, he died a horrible death. Many bullets were taken to his body at the time of his demise.

At the age of fifteen, in the year 1996, I remember that fateful morning when the echoes of gunshots whistling in the air awakened me. Upon being awake, I counted 108 bullets ringing in my ear. At midday, I heard that this head gang member had a shootout with the local and special force police officers. After the shoot out, he was wounded so badly that his body could not be recognized. Then as usual, others like him came after to slither in his shadow. Like the Bible states in 1*st Peter* 5:8, the devil walks the earth like a roaring lion seeking to devour whom he may. Do not let him catch you in disbelief for he will exploit you.

As for me, I was always sheltered from the evil deeds of others in my community. The entire community respected my grandfather. He was a very upright man, a virtual "Jack-of-all-trades" and "Master-of-all." He could do anything with his hands. Therefore, the community always needed his brawny limbs to fix or build something. Our family was sheltered from a lot of crime because of him. I truly thank him for this. God planted him to protect and watch over us. I know that God placed him in my life. As a little boy, I watched my grandfather's every move. I gazed on him like a hawk watches its prey. Talk about pride and joy; he was mine. I learned to be very ambitious, hard working, and diligent in all that I do because of his examples. God rest his soul. I love you granddad. Mr. Caleb McEnnis, thank God for you.

You might ask why I looked up to my grandfather so much, but what about my father? Well, for the first seven years of my life, my father was hardly around. I would see him every other week or on weekends. My mother was the one who worked and aided in my survival. When I was age seven, my mother was determined that she was going to give us a chance at having a better life. In order to do so, she decided to migrate to the United States. But before leaving, because of the high crime rate in my grandparents' community, my mother took my sister and me to live with our father. He lived roughly an hour away in walking distance. The four of us lived together for only a few months, and then my mother migrated to the United States in January of 1989. These were the best few months of my life. Having had both my parents under one roof was a blessing that may never happen again. This saddens me even unto this very day, but God will definitely make a way. He surely works in ways we cannot see.

My father was a Jamaican police officer. He then became the zone chief of a prominent security firm. If anyone knows anything about Jamaican police officers, one would know that it is better to be loved than hated by one. They are very stern, strict, stubborn, and just plain harsh. You read earlier about the type of men they come up against. They must stand firm. My father, however, was able to balance it all and be nice at the same time. He was, however, very hard on me. I guess he saw my talents and attributes and decided to make sure that more good than bad was rooted in me. Jamaica can be a very harsh place and peer pressure is very rampant. Do not be fooled by the tourism and all the tropical water you see on television. Jamaica is a third world country. If you are not careful, another can take your life away in the twinkling of an eye. Poverty can cause one to continuously think evil deeds. When one is truly hungry, one will do anything for food. The devil knows all this, and it is within his plan to starve the world into his kingdom. Will you resist him? The Bible states in *James* 4:7, " ... resist the devil, and he will flee from you." Again, I ask, will you resist the devil?

As stated earlier, this is the impoverished environment in which I grew up. My father's community was much better. Nice people, lots of trees, and a really low crime rate. I went to primary school then on to high school. I had many friends, but only two could ever come to my house "legally." The rest I would sneak in when my father was at work. He only liked two of my friends and I now know why. Boy, were some of the others unruly. In the midst of all that was going on, I have always loved God. I can distinctly remember that whenever I swore, had an evil thought, or did anything against God, I would always find myself saying, "God, please forgive me." One day I must have asked God to forgive me over a thousand times. I always felt bad within myself that I had to ask for forgiveness so many times. But, I always knew that I needed God in order for me to make it. I was also very smart and wanted to become a scientist. I would always mix my mother's make up and all sorts of chemicals trying to do experiments. I like to have fun in all I do. Often times my fun ended with me getting spanked by my parents.

One day I heard that scientists are very ungodly and that they will not accept the idea of creation according to the Bible in the *Book of Genesis*. I then decided that was not the route for me. I would become a doctor instead. I was only a little boy with so much passion and love for God. In reflecting back, that was amazing. Who can say that their child is this way today? I dare say only a few. This world that we are now living in is so much more sinful than the world that I was born into. Children today cannot be talked to, they know it all and can do it all. On October 26th, 1996, I migrated to the United States to live with my mother. I was so very sad, leaving my friends behind. Nevertheless, my sadness was quickly quenched, as the love for my mother was stronger than any sadness within me. I missed her deeply. I had not seen her in almost eight years. Although we spoke over the phone everyday, things were not the same. For me, emotionally it was like she never left, but I missed her physically.

I continued high school at Springfield Gardens High School in Queens, New York. At this school, shootouts in the cafeteria and outside the building between students were extensive just a few years before I started. All students had to now enter and exit the building through metal detectors. This was quite the experience for me. I came from a crime filled country to a crime filled city. Thus, sadly to say, I felt right at home. Since I was already used to this life I was able to adjust quickly. I remained focused and grounded in the principles I was taught. I stayed out of trouble and others' business. I did not gossip or bother anyone. Plus, there were a lot of Jamaicans that attended this school. I was able to make new friends quickly. I also ran into a fellow student that went to the same high school with me in Jamaica. However, we never grew close because of differences in our lifestyles.

I had only two good friends, or so I thought. I remained diligent, so my grades were still in good standing. Nonetheless, I started straying away from the principles I was taught as a youngster. My mom worked in the afternoon when I was at school and came home when I was already in "dreamland." She never really talked with me about school and how my days were going. But, she knew my two friends. A lot of things they did, I did not agree with, but I would go partying and meeting girls with them. I became sexually active before migrating to the United States. However, after migrating and meeting people, sexual immorality was all I knew. It got so bad that I no longer believed that fornication was a sin. I would tell myself that the Bible never "spoke" against having sex before marriage. My mother was completely unaware of my sexual activity. It was not her fault, work took its toll on her, and I took advantage of the situation. My mother is very industrious and worked really hard to provide for her family.

Nevertheless, I started going to a Pentecostal Church of God with my family. I remained a sinner because all I saw around me was sin. Everyone in the church had all kinds of jewelry, tattoos, clothing, and playmates. I felt right at home. Church was fun because you got to do whatever it was that you wanted to, as long as you came to praise the Lord on Sunday and brought your offering. I enjoyed the praises and the preacher's reading of the Word. I felt as though I did not have to read the Bible for myself, as I did not feel encouraged to do so.

Anyhow, I went on to Union college, in Schenectady, New York, and once again left my friends behind. There went the neighborhood. It was time to party, party, party, and fornicate. All these things are widespread on college campuses. I was never a smoker or drinker, but I sure could fornicate. My grades started slipping. I would go home on some weekends and attend church. It was still the same. In my sophomore year, my grades started falling even more and my life just felt empty. I had it all, the looks, the charm, money in my pocket, and females were everywhere. Why was I feeling so empty inside? Yes, I had family issues, but what family does not? I just felt like I was missing something, missing a great part of my life. I played rugby, I was a Residential Advisor, a part of the Protestant Ministry on campus (yes, even in my promiscuity), and a Big Brother. But, I just could not be filled anywhere, not even at church. I felt so very lost and alone.

In my junior year of college, I got baptized "in the name of the Father, Son, and, Holy Spirit, in Jesus's name," to fill my emptiness. I thought life was going to be better. I was wrong. Life only got worse. I kept on in my promiscuity with different women. There was nothing inside of me to keep me from doing these things. The Bible reads in *Acts* 1:8, the Holy Ghost gives you the power to resist. How come I did not feel any power? I had the Holy Ghost, right? The Bible also reads in *Romans* 8:11, the Holy Ghost quickens your mortal body. Where was that quickening power in me? I was missing out big time. In addition, I thought that once you accepted Jesus as your Lord and Savior, you would be saved. I am sure a lot of you that are reading were told the same thing that I was told. Yes, it is written in *Romans* 10:9–10, that if you accept Jesus as your Savior you will be saved. However, if you read the verses that follow these latter verses, you would see that it takes more than just accepting Jesus as your Lord and Savior to be saved. You must obey the gospel. A critical part of the gospel's message is in *Acts* 2:38. I will assess *Acts* 2:38 and how to be saved in the next chapter. Anyhow, while growing up, I was never taught about the importance of the Holy Spirit and speaking with other tongues as the Spirit of God gives you utterance (*Acts* 2:4). How come I did not feel any of these things after being "saved?" Something was definitely not right. I decided to stop going to church because it became a task/duty for me. What was keeping me there? I know somebody reading can relate to this question.

Anyway, in the latter part of my junior year, my grades were on the rise, but too little too late. Therefore, I decided to turn away from becoming a doctor. My grades would not cut it. I decided to remain a Biology major as that was my favorite subject. I then doubled up with Psychology as I thought being a counselor was something I could handle. I prayed night and day for God to help me through. I was about to graduate and did not know what was out there for me. Then, just before graduation two people from the New England Center for Children in Massachusetts came to recruit students to work with children with various mental and developmental disabilities. I went to the meeting and took their business card. I thought nothing of it, but I kept the card. After graduation, I worked at a summer camp at Sienna College in Loudonville, New York. Not knowing what would happen afterwards, one day I stumbled upon the business card in my drawer. I took it to the computer lab and emailed the recruiter.

She told me to come in for an interview. I went to the interview and got really interested. Nothing comes easy though. I needed a license and a car in order to do this job. I had neither. I was twenty-two years old without a license. I felt so lost once again. I prayed and started practicing to drive with Andrea Johnson, a very close friend of mine at the camp. I had two months to do all this. I told my mother about my situation and she said she would help me. We both had no money. My mother then called me a day later and said she had a friend that would sell her a car for $1,300.00.

I prayed some more. I then got the urge to go and take the written test for the driver's license. I passed. The next hurdle was to get the license. I still did not know if I had gotten the job. But, I had a lot of faith. I then called the company and told them that I had everything. I was all set to work for them. They gladly gave me an offer. I accepted. You may say I lied to them, but I say, "no," I only activated my faith. I then applied to graduate school since the company reimbursed for tuition. At this point in time, I still had no license or car. I kept on praying. I went home to New York City on a mini-vacation from the camp. I took the driver's test and passed. I drove before when I was in Jamaica, so I had some knowledge of what I was doing. You would not have found a more elated person than me on that day. Now, along with my paycheck, money from my mother, and some money borrowed from my friend Andrea, I was able to come up with the money to purchase the vehicle. I

did so and went on my merry way to Massachusetts.
I had faith, my friends.

"Now faith is the substance of things hoped
for, the evidence of things not seen" (*Hebrews* 11:1).
I had faith that I was going to get all I needed for
this job and I planned accordingly. God brought me
through.

Above all though, I was still very empty inside.
I was also accepted to the graduate counseling
program at Framingham State College. God has
blessed me with a new job and the chance to get my
master's degree. Things were rocky in both school
and work as both were life-changing experiences for
me. I somehow managed to cope by holding on to
my faith in Christ Jesus. Through all this, I still had
not received any of the things that were promised to
those who received the Holy Spirit. Could this mean
I did not have the Holy Spirit?

All the same, on March 11, 2006, I went to
purchase a new Verizon wireless cell phone. A man
that I was in line with approached me as if he knew
who I was. He told me that I looked very familiar to
him. We then started talking about our endeavors.
In the midst of our conversation, he asked me if I
attended church. I told him that I have been looking
and could not find one that was true. He then told
me about his church, the New Hope Apostolic
Church. He told me that there were some brothers
in the church that were on fire for Jesus. I started
thinking to myself, "Wow, that sounds powerful."
He then invited me to church and took my number.

His name is Jon Dyer. I went two Friday nights later and my life has not been the same since then. This is where Pastor Kurt Geddis, first ministered into my hearing about the power of the Holy Ghost.

HOW I GOT SAVED

I continued going to church. Day in and day out I would see the brothers and sisters praising the Lord with all that they had in them. I would see people rolling on the floor, running around the pews, speaking with other tongues, and shaking as if something had power over their mortal bodies. The Bible reads of such demonstrative expressions of joy for Jesus. I am not saying that we should all run around the pews and roll on the floor. But, we must praise Jesus to the fullest. I started meditating on God and reading the Bible more. I came to the realization that these people truly loved the Lord. Never in my life had I seen people praise the Lord like the Bible reads you should. The Bible also reads in *Revelation* 19:6, that people in heaven praised the Lord " … as it were the voice of a great multitude, and as the voice of many waters, and as the voice of mighty thunderings, saying, Alleluia: for the Lord God omnipotent reigneth." My God! That is a whole lot of praising. There must have been a lot of clapping, stomping, and shouting. Can your church "roar" like thunder? There is also an account in *Isaiah* 6:3–4, where the angels cried out one to another and praised the Lord until the doorposts in heaven shook and the house was filled with smoke.

Can you shake a doorpost by just praising the Lord? Lord knows my church tries to rock the walls and still cannot do it. One time we praised the Lord so vigorously until the sanctuary was filled with smoke, but the smoke came from a heater that was on the floor. We started praising the Lord even more until the smoke cleared. My friends, praise the Lord with all your might. He deserves our praise. "Let everything that hath breath praise the Lord" (*Psalm* 150:6). Also, praise Him with the trumpet, praise Him with the harp and psaltry. Praise Him with the timbrel and dancing. Praise Him with stringed instruments. Praise Him with cymbals and loud cymbals (*Psalm* 150:3-5). You must make a joyful noise unto the Lord (*Psalm* 100:1). These are not my words. These words came straight from the Bible. Brethren, there is a time when our reverence for God is manifested in quiet, controlled reflection, but when it is time to praise the Lord, we must really praise Him. *Praise ye the Lord*!

I must admit, at first I truly thought these Holy Ghost-filled people were crazy, but you should see us praise the Lord. Friends, believe me, I have not been brainwashed; if you give God the chance to manifest Himself in you, I guarantee that you will never be the same. As it is said, "When the praises go up, the blessings will come down." Anyway, let me go back to before I got saved. With all that was going through my mind, I never got discouraged. Something inside of me kept on saying, "This is right." One Friday night after church, I spoke with Brother Ronnie Johnson in the church's parking lot. The conviction about Jesus was so strong within him that it grabbed a hold of me and convicted me to be re-baptized in the name of Jesus Christ only. On my way home that same night, I called Pastor Geddis and told him that I was ready to be re-baptized in the name of the Lord Jesus Christ as the Bible reads in *Acts 2:38*. I told him that I wanted to do it on Monday, June 19, 2006. He said, "Ok, come at 9 a.m." I started thinking to myself again, "What kind of man is this that would come in to church just to baptize one person?" I love this man so much. Thank you, Jesus. Thank you for using Pastor Geddis to lead me to true Bible salvation.

That Monday morning, I went into the church located at 88 Webster Street in Worcester, Massachusetts. I got there at 9:15 a.m. Brother Gbarwea came to assist the pastor. This brother loves the Lord with all that is in him. I changed my clothing and sat down with both men. Pastor Geddis then read *Romans chapter* 6 to me. Part of this chapter reads, "Know ye not that so many of us as were baptized into Jesus Christ were baptized into His death?" Friends, this is the significance of baptism; we die with Jesus, our sins are buried with Him, and then we rise from the water (which represents His blood) to walk in the newness of life. Can you see the parallel here? Jesus shed His blood and died on the cross, was buried in the tomb, He then rose from the dead to a new and eternal life. Do you want to live forever? Follow the formula.

Pastor Geddis then asked me if I truly believed that Jesus is my Lord and Savior and that He died for my sins. I honestly replied, "Yes, sir." Pastor Geddis then took me to the baptismal pool. I went in. Man, was the water cold. I started quivering like I had never quivered in my life. Pastor Geddis then prayed and immersed me under the water in the name of Jesus Christ. He then let go of my head and my body floated up out of the water. I have now been baptized in the name of my Lord and Savior Jesus Christ. While still in the water, I tried touching the bottom of the pool, but my legs just kept floating up. My body felt strange as if I had no control. I started praising the Lord shouting, "Alleluia, fill me Lord, fill me today!" Pastor Geddis then laid his hand on my head, my mouth flew open, and I started quickening and speaking with other tongues. I had no idea what came over me. I started crying and praising the Lord at the same time.

My feet still kept on floating, I just could not sit still on the little built-in bench in the pool. My whole body started floating. Listen, I tried floating at the beach before and I could not do it to save my life. Pastor then lead me out of the pool and stood me up. My body started moving in ways I could not control. I kept on speaking with other tongues with my head bowed. I straightened my head and my whole body bowed down. I straightened my body and it bowed again. I had no power over my body. I started crying and asking, "What is happening to me?" Pastor then replied, "Do not fight it, just let God have His way." After about twenty minutes, Brother Gbarwea ran like a mad man to the first pew. He started singing in other tongues. Yes, you read right, that brother was under the first pew on his back singing to the Lord with other tongues. He is from Liberia, but the language he was uttering was not from his home country. I then said, "My God, I want to be like that brother."

From that day on, I kept on reading the Bible, going to church, staying on fire, and praising the Lord with all that is in me. I want to be ready when Jesus comes. I want to go to heaven. Do you? My God, my God, look where you have brought me from. In the name of Jesus, I thank you.

2.

The oneness of God and how one can be saved

HIS NAME

Hear, O Israel: The Lord our God is one Lord ... love the Lord thy God with all thine heart, all thy soul, and with all thy might (*Deuteronomy* 6:4–5). My fellow beings, our Lord and Savior is but one God. There are not three gods. Jesus encompasses them all. There is no God the Father, God the Son, and God the Holy Spirit. Jesus is the Father in Creation (*John* 1:10 *and Isaiah* 9:6), the Son in redemption (*John* 3:16–17), and the Holy Ghost in the church (*John* 14:20, 26–27, *and Acts* 9:31). Hence, there is no *Trinity*. He is but one and His name is Jesus Christ. "In Him dwelleth all the fullness of the *Godhead* bodily. And ye are complete in Him, which is the head of all principality and power (*Colossians* 2:9)." For this reason we are called by His name. We are Christ-like. My friends, we are Christians. The Godhead, according to the 1997 *version of the Merriam-Webster's dictionary* is the divine nature or essence of God especially as existing in three persons. What is a person? An individual, one of the three parts of being in the Godhead as understood by Trinitarians. What is the Trinity? This is the unity of

Father, Son, and Holy Spirit as three persons in the Godhead.

Now, in looking at these three definitions from the same dictionary as above, it seems here that Trinitarians believe that there are three gods. A friend of mine who also believes in the Trinity said that the Godhead consists of three gods with one purpose and one like mind. If we are supposed to be a monotheistic religion, does this make sense? It seems here that there are three gods. Well, the Bible tells me that there is but one God. Where does the Bible read about the Trinity? I know that Jesus is God. Thus, the next time a person that follows the Trinity says that he does not believe in three gods, ask him to explain his doctrine to you, for it is very confusing to me. I repeat, *Jesus* is *God! See Acts* 9:4–5.

In *Isaiah* 43:10–11, the Bible reads, "Ye are my witnesses, saith the Lord, and my servant whom I have chosen: that ye may know and believe me, and understand that I am He: before me there was no God formed, neither shall there be after me. I, even I, am the Lord; and beside me there is no saviour." He continued in *verse* 12 by saying, "I have declared, and have saved, and I have shewed, when there was no strange god among you: therefore ye are my witnesses, saith the Lord, that I am God." Do you still believe that Jesus is not God? We all know that Jesus came down from heaven and died for our sins, right? We also believe that Jesus is our Lord and Savior, right? Well, God said in *verse* 11 above, " … I am the Lord, and beside me there is no saviour."

The *Book of Isaiah* is in the Old Testament, therefore, Jesus did not knowingly come to earth yet as these words were written.

To further illustrate that Jesus is God as well as the Son of God, in 1*st Timothy* 3:16, Paul states, " ... Without controversy great is the mystery of godliness: God was manifested in the flesh, justified in the Spirit, seen of angels, preached unto the Gentiles, believed on in the world, received up into glory." OK, the beginning of the latter verse states, "without controversy." This simply means that this claim cannot be disputed. There are no opposing views to this statement. The Word has spoken. Then came, "great is the mystery of godliness." No matter how smart we think we are; we will never understand the omnipresence of God. He can be in me, you, in heaven, and down the street at the same time and still be one. Our thoughts and the thoughts of God are like the distance from the earth to heaven (*Isaiah* 55:8–9). My friends, stop trying to understand the Word and just do and believe what is written by faith.

Please do not get caught up in trying to comprehend God. You never will. God was manifested in the flesh and preached unto the Gentiles. Jesus was the only one who came in the flesh and preached to the Gentiles. This shows that He is God. You see, God is a Spirit as Jesus Himself stated in *John* 4:24. You cannot see a spirit. This is why He came down in the flesh and lead a life of example to which we must follow and adhere to. He prayed to His Father in heaven many times as to show us how to pray to

Him. Not to Him in the flesh on earth, but to Him in heaven. "I and my Father are one" (*John* 10:30). Jesus in the flesh was praying to Jesus, the Spirit. Let it sink in.

To discover more about the oneness of God, read *Hebrews* 6:13, *James* 2:19, 1*st John* 5:7, *John* 1:1 *and* 14, *Revelation* 1:8, and *Revelation* 4:2, where John said, " ... Behold, a throne was set in heaven, and one sat on the throne." My friends, this chapter is self-explanatory, the man of God has spoken. For He who dwells in the secret place of the most High shall protect me, He shall be my guide, my help cometh from Him, He gives us victory over death, and gives us triumph over our adversary. He, Jesus, is our God and at His name, all knees shall bow and all tongues shall confess that He is Lord (*Philippians* 2:10–11). Yes friends, you, the angels, and I will all submit to the will of Jesus when he returns. Alleluia!

Being Saved By Baptism In Jesus's Name

"For God so loved the world that He gave His only begotten Son, that whosoever believeth in Him should not perish, but have everlasting life" (*John* 3:16). After obtaining help from God, I **clearly** provided evidence that Jesus is God. So now the question is, how can one truly be saved? My friends, one can only be saved through the blood of Jesus Christ. In *John* 14:6, Jesus said, " ... I am the way, the truth, and the life: no man cometh unto the Father but, by me." The only way is through baptism in the name of Jesus Christ. There is only one way. In *Matthew* 16:16, Peter confessed that Jesus is Christ, Son of the living God. Jesus then said in *verses* 18–19, " ... thou art Peter, and upon this rock I will build my church; and the gates of hell shall not prevail against it. I will give unto thee the keys of the kingdom of heaven: and whatsoever thou shalt bind on earth shall be bound in heaven: and whatsoever thou shalt loose on earth shall be loosed in heaven." You may be asking yourself right now, "What is so relevant about this verse?" Let me tell you its relevance. Jesus, who is God, gave Peter, who would remain on earth the keys to heaven. Through Jesus Christ, Peter now has control of whom he should loose to the kingdom of God.

Now, in *Acts chapter* 2, on the day of Pentecost when the apostles received the Holy Ghost and were speaking with other tongues, a multitude that heard all the noise came among them in disbelief. Peter, with the other eleven apostles, then stood and spoke with the people thoroughly about the goodness of Jesus. People who became pricked in their hearts by the Word then asked Peter and the rest of the apostles what they should do to be saved. In *verse* 38 of the latter *chapter*, Peter, who has the key to heaven then said unto them, "Repent and be baptized every one of you in the name of Jesus Christ for the remission of sins, and ye shall receive the gift of the Holy Ghost." In *verse* 40, Peter also told the people to " ... save [themselves] from this [perverse] generation." After his speech, three thousand souls that gladly received the Word of God were all baptized. Another reason it is imperative that we listen to Peter is because Jesus told Peter three times to feed His sheep if he loves Him (*John* 21:15–17). We are the sheep and Jesus is the Shepherd (*John* 10:11). Peter is trying to feed us in *Acts chapter* 2. Do you want to be fed? I know I surely do. Are you not hungry for Jesus? Be fed! The choice is yours to be filled with this "happy meal" in Jesus.

Nevertheless, like I wrote before, one can only be saved by being washed in the blood of Jesus Christ (*Revelation 7:9–14*). The water represents the blood of Jesus. In *John 3:5 and 7*, Jesus said, " ... Except a man be born of water and of the Spirit, he cannot enter into the kingdom of God ... Ye must be born again." Additionally, "He that believeth and is baptized shall be saved; but he that believeth not shall be damned ... these signs shall follow them that believe; in my name ... they shall speak with new tongues ... " (*Mark* 16:16–17).

Romans chapter 6 further reveals why we baptize in Jesus's name.

> ... How shall we, that are dead to sin, live any longer therein? Know ye not, that so many of us as were baptized into Jesus Christ were baptized into His death? Therefore we are buried with Him by baptism into death: that like as Christ was raised up from the dead by the glory of the Father, even so we also should walk in the newness of life. For if we have been planted together in the likeness of His death, we shall be also in the likeness of His resurrection ... our old man is crucified with Him, that the body of sin might be destroyed

> ... for He that is dead is freed
> from sin.
>
> *(Romans 6:2–7)*

My brethren, you must die with Christ in order to live with Christ. You must be washed clean. Think about this once more, Christ died, was buried, and then rose from the dead. This is what Paul is telling us that we must do in *Roman's chapter* 6. We must first die to sin by repenting and being buried in the watery grave by baptism in Jesus' name. Then we must rise from that watery grave where we are now dead to sin, and walk in the newness of life in Christ. " ... For if we be dead with Him, we shall also live with Him: if we suffer, we shall also reign with Him ... If we believe not, yet he abideth faithful: He cannot deny Himself " *(2nd Timothy* 2:11–13). People, this is straight from the Bible. Acknowledge the Word of God! He that has an ear let him hear what the Lord says.

So, how can we die with Christ? The only way is to die in His name. Baptism comes from the Greek word *baptizo*, which means, to be immersed or dipped into. Being sprinkled about the head with water is not baptism. One must be buried or immersed completely into the water in the name of Christ Jesus, emerging to walk in the newness of life. Hence, we are called Christians. So, if you have not repented of your sins, accepted Christ as your Lord and Savior, were or are not baptized in the name of Jesus Christ only, and have not received the Holy

Ghost, you are not saved; neither are you a Christian, and hellfire shall be your domain. These are not my words. These words are from the Bible. Just keep reading with an open heart and Jesus will guide your thoughts. The disciples were first called Christians in Antioch (*Acts* 11:26). They were of Jesus; they preached about Him through the apostles' doctrine (*Acts* 2:42), they believed only in Him as their Savior, all preached about baptism in Jesus's name, and they all had the gift of the Holy Ghost with the evidence of speaking with other tongues as the Spirit of God gave them utterance (*Acts* 2:4). Friends, I only speak the truth in love (*Ephesians* 4:15).

You may be asking yourself two questions at this point.

What about the unsaved thief on the cross who went to heaven that very day when he asked Jesus to remember him (*Luke* 23:42–43)? Jesus was not glorified then (*John* 7:39). His blood was shed but He was not dead to sin yet (*Romans* 6:10). Thus, baptism in Jesus's name and the Holy Ghost were not a requirement to *reach heaven* as of that moment. Plus, in *Romans* 9:15, Paul wrote, " ... [God] saith to Moses, I will have mercy and compassion on whom I wish to have compassion." Come on, people, He is God. He is the One who made the heaven, the earth, you, and me. He tells us what to do and not vice versa. If God states that the only way to be saved is through baptism in His name and receiving the Holy Ghost, other than Him having mercy because of your contrite heart, then you must take heed. Do you know if He will have mercy on you? Be baptized! Even John the Baptist's disciples were re-baptized in the name of the Lord Jesus and when Paul laid his hands on them, they received the Holy Ghost (*Acts* 19:1–6). Furthermore, remember the Ethiopian Eunuch whom God made a way in the desert for him to be baptized (*Acts* 8:26–39)? If God made a way for just one soul to be baptized, what about you? Are you too good to be baptized in the name of the Lord Jesus? My friends, I know that I do not know anything except what is written. Thus, I am going to abide by every Word that has proceeded from God in the Bible.

The second question you may ask is, "What about *Matthew* 28:19?" In this verse, Jesus gave the great commandment stating, "Go ye therefore, and teach all nations, baptizing them in the *Name* of the Father, and of the Son, and of the Holy Ghost." Here the name is singular; plus we know that the Father, the Son, and the Holy Ghost is Jesus Christ Himself. You cannot limit God to three distinct manifestations to humanity. God is also the author and the finisher of our faith (*Hebrews* 12:2), He is the Head of the church (*Ephesians* 5:23), He is the only begotten Son (*John* 3:16), He is the everlasting Father (*Isaiah* 9:6), He is the Savior (*John* 4:42), He is the Lord of lords (1*st Timothy* 6:15), the Alpha and the Omega (*Revelation* 22:13), and He is the Amen (*Revelation* 3:14). His name is Jesus and He shall save *His* people from their sins (*Matthew* 1:21 *and* 25). Additionally, His name *Emmanuel* means God with us (*Matthew*

1:23). There is no power in the Trinity, none! The power is in the name of Jesus (*1st Corinthians* 5:4).

Furthermore, Father is not the name of a person, neither is Son, nor the Holy Ghost. These are titles of a person. I am a son and soon I hope to be a father. My name is LeeRoy, not son. If you want to talk about the names of God, let us go back to the Old Testament a bit. I am going to show you few of the names of God and what they mean. Then I am going to further show you why you need to be baptized in Jesus's name. God's names are as follows: El Shaddai: "God Almighty" (*Genesis* 17:1), El Elyon: "The Most High God" (*Deuteronomy* 26:19), El Roi: "The God who sees" (*Genesis* 16:13), Elohim: "One God and God the creator" (*Genesis* 1:1), Adonai: "The Lord God" (*Genesis* 15:2), JEHOVAH: "Lord God Almighty" (*Exodus* 6:3), JEHOVAH-Jireh: "The Lord will provide" (*Genesis* 22:14), JEHOVAH-Rophe: "The Lord of healing" (*Exodus* 15:26), JEHOVAH-Nissi: "The Lord is my banner" (*Exodus* 17:15), JEHOVAH-M'Kaddesh: "The Lord who sanctifies" (*Leviticus* 20:8), JEHOVAH-Shalom: "The Lord is peace" (*Judges* 6:24), JEHOVAH-Tsidkenu: "The God of righteousness" (*Jeremiah* 23:5), JEHOVAH-Rohi: "The Lord our Shepherd" (*Psalm* 23:1), JEHOVAH-Sabaoth: "The Lord of Hosts" (*Isaiah* 1:24), JEHOVAH-Shammah: "The Lord is there" (*Ezekiel* 48:35), and Jesus: "The God of Salvation" (*Mathew* 1:21). There are many other names of God. These names merely came about because people did not know God's true name. Hence, they called Him many. However, His name is Jesus and it is the only name that can save us from our sins (*Acts* 4:12). The name Jesus is exalted above every name (*Philippians* 2:9). Friends, Jesus was sent to earth to take on our sins (*Hebrews* 9:28). For this reason, we must put on His name through baptism (*Galatians* 3:13–29). When you are baptized in the name of Jesus, you are taking on Christ Himself and you are now His redeemed (*Galatians* 3:27). Along with receiving the Holy Ghost, this is how one becomes a Christian. Again, God has spoken, not I. Just keep reading. Amen!

Peter, who understood the fulfillment of what Jesus said in *Matthew* 28:19, told us how to truly be baptized. Jesus is a jealous God (*Exodus* 34:14), not a vain one. He did not say, "Go baptize in my name," because He did not want to give glory to Himself in the flesh (*Philippians* 2:5–8 *and Hebrews* 5:5); but to speak of He, the Father of creation and the "Son of man" (*Matthew* 20:28), who abides in heaven. If this perplexes your brain, I truly do understand. It baffles my brain too, but I am going by faith and not by sight. In *Ephesians* 4:4–6, Paul wrote, "There is one body, and one Spirit … one Lord, one faith, one baptism, one God and Father of all who is above all and through all, and in you all." My friends, I pray that God gives us all wisdom. So, "[Until] we all come in the unity of the faith, and of the knowledge of the Son of God … " (*Ephesians* 4:13), I am going to witness of Him. People, have faith in Christ. Believe on Him. Faith, faith, faith, just a little bit of faith is what you need for " ... without faith it is impossible to please God" (*Hebrews* 11:6). The grace of God be with you all.

BEING SAVED BY THE POWER OF THE HOLY GHOST

Just like the wind that keeps on blowing, you cannot see it but you feel it move. So is the Holy Ghost like the wind (*John* 3:8). I can feel the Holy Ghost move within me, while my body quickens all over on the outside. In chapter one of this book, I mentioned how the power of Holy Ghost feels when He moves so deep within my soul. Now, let us see what the Bible reads about what I feel. The Holy Ghost is the Spirit of Christ who is the ever-living God. In *John* 14:16, Jesus said to His disciples, " … I will pray the Father, and He shall give you another comforter that He may abide with you forever." Another comforter? Well, Jesus is the first comforter because He has been there for His disciples. They had been through much together and they believed on Him wholeheartedly. He strengthened and comforted them through all their perils. Am I right? So, now that Jesus is about to leave them, He said that He would send another comforter.

Who is this comforter? Jesus Himself cleared this up in *John* 14:26–27 when He said, "But the comforter which is the Holy Ghost, whom the Father will send in my name, He shall teach you all things, and bring all things to your remembrance ... peace I leave with you, my peace I give you; not as the world giveth, give I unto you." My God, this feels soothing; my very own comforter from God Himself. What more can I ask for? Jesus also stated that, "Even the Spirit of truth; whom the world cannot receive, because it seeth nor knoweth Him not: but ye know Him; for He dwelleth with you, and shall be in you" (*John* 14:17). "He shall be in you?" Does this mean that the comforter who is the Holy Ghost as well as Jesus Christ and God comes to live in you? Yes, my friends. God wants to live inside you. That is why we must stay free from sin, so that God Almighty can have a place to dwell. He wants to love us more, He wants to talk with us, He wants to walk with us, and He wants our body for His own glory and purpose. You do not believe me? See *Verse* 20 of this same chapter when Jesus said, " ... I am in my Father and [my Father] in me, and I in you." How Jesus lives in me and in heaven at the same time I may never know.

All I know is when the Spirit moves upon me I am clueless as to what is going on within me. I just know that it feels mighty good and all I can do is praise Him in a dance, like King David danced before the Lord with all his might until his garments fell off (*2nd Samuel* 6:14 *and* 20). I can never deny that Jesus is in me. I truly feel His quickening power all day long. My body is in constant motion. I simply cannot keep still and my heart is as calm as can be. This means that it is not my adrenaline that is flowing. My mind cannot even detect what is flowing. All I truly know is that the Bible reads, "Quench not the Spirit" (1*st Thessalonians* 5:19). I just cannot keep quiet. I have to give God all the praises and honor when He moves inside me. I get so excited when I talk about Jesus. I just get so excited when I think about all He has done for me, and how He has also made me free. My friends, I just get so excited and I cannot be in silence. I must tell it, I must testify about the goodness of my Jesus. Amen!

Now, the question is, how do you know that you have the Holy Ghost? In *Acts* 2:1–5, on the day of *Pentecost*, which is a Hebrew festival annually celebrated fifty days after Passover (*Exodus* 12:21–28), the Bible reads, " ... when the day of Pentecost was fully come, [the Apostles and other followers of Christ] were with one accord in one place ... suddenly there came a sound from heaven as a rushing mighty wind, and it filled all the house where they were sitting ... there appeared unto them cloven tongues like as of fire, and it sat upon each of them ... they were all filled with the Holy Ghost, and began to speak with other tongues as the Spirit gave them utterance." Speaking with other tongues as the Spirit gives you utterance is the initial evidence of the Holy Ghost. There are other gifts of tongues like the *Book of Corinthians* reads about, which is not for everyone. However, the initial tongue, which is the evidence of the reception of the Holy Ghost, is a " ... promise unto you and your children, and to all that are afar off, even as many as the Lord our God shall call" (*Acts* 2:39). The latter scripture was first penned by the prophet Joel (*Joel* 2:28–29). Believe me, my friends. This is real. The Holy Ghost in me is constantly guiding me to all truth about God (*John* 16:13). I would not be writing a book about my experience with Christ and the Holy Ghost if He were not real.

I shared with you what happened on the day of and after I received the Holy Ghost. I lie not. I know some of you grew up in churches where you see people rolling on the floor and speaking other languages and it is scary. I was there too. I never believed it. Plus, of course you know that some people fake it. However, think about this, people fake what they know they should have. You cannot fake something that does not exist. You mimic what is real, right? So, the fact that some people fake the Holy Ghost is also evidence that He is real. Think about it.

The *Book of Romans, chapter* 8 further illustrates what the Holy Ghost feels like and His whole purpose in our mortal bodies. This chapter starts by reading in *verse* 1, "There is no condemnation to them which are in Christ Jesus, who walk not after the flesh, but after the Spirit." *Verses* 3 *and* 5 then read, " ... God sending His Son in the likeness of sinful flesh, and for sin, condemned sin in the flesh. For they that are after the flesh do mind the things of the flesh but they that are after the Spirit, the things of the Spirit" *Verse* 8 then reads, " ... they that are in the flesh cannot please God." You need the Holy Ghost to please God. If you want the things of this world and always want to please the flesh, then you are hindering yourself from pleasing God. Did you know that there are only a few enemies of God and that the flesh is one of them? The world is another and we all know that the archenemy is the devil. I will talk more about these enemies of God in a later chapter. Right now I am going to tell you the purpose of the Holy Ghost in you. We do not know what our heart desires. We may think we do, but we never will. Only God knows this.

The Holy Ghost " ... maketh intercession for us with groanings which cannot be uttered ... and He that searcheth the hearts knoweth what is the mind of the Spirit, because He maketh intercession for the saints according to the will of God" (*Romans* 8:26–27). I too find myself groaning uncontrollably when I pray. This especially happens when I am praying for something that I am in need of or praying for someone in need and my heart is heavy. My God, I can honestly say that I can relate to this scripture and all that it reads. You that are reading and think that you have the Holy Ghost/Spirit in you, can you honestly relate? Can you relate to the quickening power of the Holy Spirit? You may ask, "Quickening power, what is that?" Well, " ... if the Spirit of Him that raised Jesus from the dead dwells in you, He that raised up Christ from the dead shall also quicken your mortal bodies by His Spirit that dwelleth in you" (*Romans* 8:11). My friends, as I was writing just now, my body was quickening/shaking so hard that at this present moment I have a little backache. Now that is the power of God. Do you have this power?

Well, you need that quickening power in order to get to the streets of gold, the place where abides the tree of life on both sides of the river (*Revelation* 22:2). I tell you the truth, "For as many of us that are led by the Spirit of God, they are the sons of God" (*Romans* 8:14). Plus, " ... if any man have not the Spirit of Christ, he is none of His" (*Romans* 8:9). You must be baptized in His name to be freed from sin and then you must receive the Holy Ghost to be His. One cannot go without the other. You need both to be saved *(John* 3:5). If this is not the case, you are not dead to sin like Christ is; neither are you children of Christ. You, my friends belong to the world, which is ruled by the devil. You can try to dispute what I write, but you can never dispute the Word of God. Let God be true and every man a liar (*Romans* 3:4). God made us, but because of sin, we have to be washed whiter than snow in order to go back to Him muck free and new.

Remember in *Matthew* 13:30, Jesus stated that the wheat and the tares would grow together until the day of harvest. The tares will be piled and burned and the wheat will be kept. The latter scripture definitely is referring to the children with the Spirit of God versus the children who have not the Spirit of God on the Day of Judgment. Can you refute this claim? It makes a lot of sense to be baptized in Jesus's name. He is the one who died for us. He died for our sins.

Thus, the evidence that He is in us is the quickening power of the Holy Ghost and speaking with other tongues. How else would you know that you have His Spirit? I cannot tell just by looking in the mirror. I need evidence.

God could have chosen another way as evidence of His Spirit if He had deemed so, but He chose speaking with other tongues. Why the tongue you may ask? Well, the Bible reads, " ... the tongue is a fire, a world of iniquity: so is the tongue among our members, that it defileth our whole body, and setteth on fire the course of nature; and it is set on fire of hell" (*James* 3:6). No man can discipline his tongue. It is " ... an unruly evil, full of deadly poison" (*James* 3:8). Thus, if God can control your tongue, He can control what you do and say. For this reason He chose the tongue. If you know not what you are saying in the Spirit, then you definitely will not know what you are doing in the Spirit and God can use you for His own purpose. That is what He wants. He wants to use you in a way where the flesh cannot interfere. My friends, how God revealed these scriptures to me, I know not. I am just a common man like you. A common man with the true Spirit of God dwelling on the inside working on the outside. Oh, what a delight in my life! All this makes sense to me and I hope that what I write makes or will make sense to you as well. In Jesus's name I pray, Amen.

There are some scriptures in the Old Testament that prophesied about the Holy Ghost. One such scripture is *Isaiah* 28:11–12, where Isaiah stated,

"For with stammering lips and another tongue will He speak to His people ... this is the refreshing: yet they would not hear." People, you must listen to the Word, you must hear God. Without the Spirit of God, you will not receive the things of God. You that are natural beings cannot understand the things of the Spirit. As stated in *1st Corinthians* 2:14–15, " ... the natural man receiveth not the things of the Spirit of God: for they are foolish unto him: neither can he know them, because they are spiritually discerned or known." The Holy Ghost giveth unto us the mind of Christ (*1st Corinthians* 2:16). Once again, these are not my words. These are the words of God. You need the Holy Ghost with the evidence of speaking with other tongues as the Spirit gives you utterance. God hath given to each man a measure of faith (*Romans* 12:3). So, " ... be not wise in your own conceits" (*Romans* 12:16). You do not have to listen to me, but you better listen to God. Remember, eight people were saved in the days of Noah (*2nd Peter* 2:5). God does not need any of us. He can wipe away this whole world and form another just like that. Take heed. I cannot save you and neither can you save me. Every man must give an account to God for himself (*Romans* 14:10–12). Please be wise and live for Jesus because *you cannot save yourself.*

One last evidence that the Spirit abides in us are the fruits of the Spirit. As stated in *Galatians* 5:22–23, " ... the fruits of the Spirit is love, joy, peace, longsuffering, gentleness, goodness, faith, meekness, temperance: against such, there is no law." My friends,

I was a bad boy. I was cocky, lustful, arrogant to some extent, and disliked people because I thought people were mostly bad and out for themselves. I mean, think about the life I experienced as a youngster. Thus, when Jesus truly came into my life, He brought along peace, He brought love, He brought joy, He brought goodness, He brought meekness, and He brought me faith. Now, I am a living proof that true churches of Christ have benefits regarding your soul. Jesus is alive and well! He lives within my heart, mind, body, and soul. Hence, He dwells in me. My friends, I will now close this chapter, but before I do, I just want you to know that Jesus loves you and I love you too. Jesus is the only way to heaven. "For by one Spirit are we baptized into one body, whether we be Jews or Gentiles … " (1*st Corinthians* 12:13). God bless.

3.

The wages of sin

THE TEN COMMANDMENTS

Ten Commandments

And God spake all these words, saying, I am the Lord
*   thy God ...*
Thou shalt have no other gods before me
Thou shalt not make unto thee any graven image
Thou shalt not take the name of the Lord thy God in
*   vain*
Remember the Sabbath day to keep it Holy
Honour thy father and thy mother
Thou shalt not kill
Thou shalt not commit adultery
Thou shalt not steal
Thou shalt not bear false witness against thy neighbour
Thou shalt not covet.

                                    (*Exodus* 20:3-17)

These are ten of the commandments of the covenant the Lord made with the children of Israel through Moses when they were brought out of bondage in Egypt. All these commandments apply to every man except for the day on which the Sabbath is observed. I will tell you why later in this very chapter. "My son keep thy father's commandments, and forsake not the law of thy mother: Bind them continually upon thine heart, and tie them about thy neck. When thou goest, it shall lead thee; when thou sleepest, it shall keep thee ... for the commandment is a lamp and the law is light ... to keep thee from evil ... " (*Proverbs* 6:20–24). Take heed, for "whoso despiseth the Word shall be destroyed: but he that feareth the commandment shall be rewarded" (*Proverbs* 13:13). These commandments are the law and are very important. He that is guilty of one is guilty of all (*James* 2:10). Jesus Himself even said, "He that hath my commandments, and keepeth them, he it is that loveth me ... and I will love Him and manifest myself to him" (*John* 14:21).

Now concerning the Sabbath, Gentiles are not under the law, we are under the period of grace. Such things as circumcision and the Sabbath do not apply to us. This has been an ongoing battle between the apostles, the scribes, and the Pharisees. " ... There rose up certain of the sect of the Pharisees which believed, saying, that it was needful to circumcise [the Gentiles] and command them to keep the Law of Moses. And the apostles and elders came together for to consider of this matter" (*Acts* 15:5–6). This must have been very important for it to be debated upon by the apostles and the elders.

> ... When there had been much
> disputing, Peter rose up, and

said unto them ... ye know
how that a good while ago God
made choice among us, that the
Gentiles by my mouth should
hear the word of the gospel, and
believe. And God ... bare them
witness, giving them the Holy
Ghost, even as He did unto us;
and put no difference between us
and them, purifying their hearts
by faith ... why tempt ye God,
to put a yoke upon the neck of
the [followers of Christ], which
neither our fathers nor we were
able to bear? ... we believe that
through the grace of the Lord
Jesus Christ we shall be saved,
even as they.

(Acts 15:7–11*)*

"Wherefore my sentence is, that we trouble not
them, which from among the Gentiles are turned to
God: But that we write unto them, that they abstain
from pollutions of idols, and from fornication, and
from things strangled, and from blood *(Acts* 15:19–
20*)*." These are the four divine rules emphasized by
the apostles that the Gentiles must adhere to as well
as common laws against such things as murdering,
stealing, killing, and so on.

The Sabbath day and circumcision were not
a part of the four divine rules above. Both were

covenants made between God and the Israelites for the children of Israel to remember what the Lord had done for them. You see, Jesus said in *Mark* 2:27, " ... The Sabbath was made for man, and not man for the Sabbath." What is your take on this? All I know is that it is good for any day to be a day of spiritual observance (*Romans* 14:5–6). Christians should be faithful to church services on any given day they are held (*Hebrews* 10:25). Even Paul preached to the disciples when they all got together on Sunday, the first day of the week (*Acts* 20:7). Saints and friends, Gentiles are not under the Mosaic Laws, but are covered by the blood of Jesus (*Colossians* 2:9–17 *and Galatians* 3:13–29). The Sabbath is a time of rest, but Jesus said, "Come unto me, all ye that labour and are heavy laden, and I will give you rest" (*Matthew* 11:28). The Holy Ghost will give you rest. We worship mainly on Sundays because Jesus rose from the dead on the first day of the week (*Mathew* 28:1–6). Thus, this day was the beginning of the New Testament church. As for circumcision, we should be circumcised of the heart (*Romans* 2:29). My friends, we must have the right spirit and a purely cleaned heart in order to make it to heaven (*Psalm* 51:10).

I will also not get caught up in the worshiping of the sun god through the time period of Emperor Constantine and how he changed the Sabbath to Sunday due to Pagan rituals. All that is irrelevant. For any day is good for worshiping the Lord. I worship Jesus from Sunday to Saturday, I know no sun god. Alleluia! All praises to Jehovah, my rock, my sword, and my shield. Thank God that I am not under the Mosaic Laws of being stoned for something as simple as being hardheaded. See *Joshua chapter 7*, where a whole family was stoned to death and then got burned because of one son being hardheaded. Wow, I would have been dead before I was even born. I came out the womb a hardheaded child. Thank God for the blood of Jesus that resides here on earth, protecting all who are saved (*1st John* 5:8). You should be thankful as well, if you are truly saved. My fellow Gentiles, we do not have to follow the Saturday Sabbath, but if you want to, it is OK, just live holy in the process and do not only worship the Lord on one day. God bless.

SIN

Lord, prepare me to be a sanctuary, one that is pure, holy and true. Lord, I want to be a sanctuary for you. This is a wonderful song that I hold so near and dear to my heart. Please Lord, use me, do not refuse me. Use me as a vessel for thee. I want God to prepare me. I want Him to use me for His Glory. You that are reading and following me, do you see what I am getting at? What is the topic of this chapter? Ok, I am going to as they say, "spill the beans." Do you want God to use you? Do you want to be a sanctuary for Jesus? Are your garments clean and ready? Are they whiter than snow? Will God continue to use a sinner as a vessel? I believe He can use a sinner for a testimony of His greatness, just as how He used Saul, who later became Paul to change the lives of many (*Acts* 9:15). However, notice what God did to Saul? He cleansed Him. He washed him and sent him on his way to sin no more (*Acts* 9:18). God hates sin. If you want to be a vessel for Christ, you need to be broken and made holy! You need to be washed whiter than snow by the precious blood of the Lamb. Alleluia!

King David penned the scripture,

> Blessed is the man that walketh not in the counsel of the ungodly, nor standeth in the way of sinners, nor sitteth in the seat of the scornful. But his delight is in the law of the Lord; and in his law doth he meditate day and night. And he shall be like a tree planted by the rivers of water, that bringeth forth his fruit in his season; his leaf also shall not wither; and whatsoever he doeth shall prosper. The ungodly are not so: but are like the chaff which the wind driveth away ... the Lord knoweth the way of the righteous; but the way of the ungodly shall perish.
>
> (*Psalm* 1:1–6)

Now, what does it mean to be ungodly? It is very plain. To be ungodly is to stray away from the things of God. Thus, when one strays away from the things of God there is nothing to prevent one from sinning. Straying away from the things of God in itself is a sin. One becomes filled with pride and feels as though one does not need God. Follow me, this will all come together as I write and you read.

Let us talk about sin. What is sin? "All unrighteousness is sin ... " (1*st John* 5:17). Thus, if you do anything that displeases God and fail to do what He commands, you are a sinner. Sin is sweet, sin is glamorous; sin can take you to the pinnacle of this world. Rappers, actors, ballers, athletes, the media, and all in the limelight who are very wealthy and filled with pride feel as though all is and will be well. Everyone has diamonds, pearls, bling bling, whips, and kicks, but no Holy Ghost. They do not even care to know who the Holy Ghost is and what He feels like. My friends, " ... the [price] of sin is death ... " (*Romans* 6:23). If you commit sin and keep on sinning, you are going to die. Do you believe that if you die a sinner you will be in paradise with God? If you believe so, then you have been duped by the devil. " ... The fearful, the unbelieving, the abominable, murderers, whoremongers, sorcerers, idolaters, and all liars shall have their part in the lake which burneth with fire and brimstone ... " (*Revelation* 21:8*)*. "Therefore do not let sin reign in your mortal body, that you should obey in its lusts ... do not present your members as instruments of unrighteousness to sin ... present yourselves ... and your members as instruments of righteousness to God. For sin shall not have dominion over you ... " (*Romans* 6:12–14, nkjv*)*.

Sin is a terrible thing. It came into the world among men when Adam and Eve sinned by disobeying God (*Genesis* 2:17, *and Romans* 5:12). Yes, my friends, disobeying God is the same as being ungodly, because you stray from the things of God. "Let no man deceive you with vain words: for because of [sin] cometh the wrath of God upon the children of disobedience" (*Ephesians* 5:6). Cain was the third to sin against God. He murdered his brother Abel and sin has existed in every generation since then. See *Genesis chapters* 3 *and* 4 for the complete story of Adam, Eve, and the demise of Abel through the cruelty of his brother, Cain (*Genesis* 4:8). I am not here to judge Cain, but killing ones' own flesh and blood is a dreadful thing. What can cause one to be so angry that he would take another's life? I pray that God will sustain me and hold on to my heart that I may not sin against Him, for I know that I cannot sustain without His help. Can you? I want to be like King David. I want to " ... keep thy statutes: O forsake me not Lord. Wherewithal shall a young man cleanse his way? by taking heed thereto according to thy word. With my whole heart have I sought thee: O let me not wander from thy commandments. Thy word have I hid in mine heart, that I might not sin against thee ... blessed art thou, O Lord: teach me thy statutes" (*Psalm* 119: 8–12).

TYPES OF SINS

In *Proverbs chapter 6:16–19*, Solomon states, "These six things doth the Lord hate; yea, seven are an abomination unto Him." The seven things are as follows:

1. *A proud look*
2. *A lying tongue*
3. *Hands that shed innocent blood*
4. *A heart that devises wicked imaginations*
5. *Feet that be swift in running to mischief*
6. *A false witness that speaks lies*
7. *And he that sows discord among brethren*

My friends, these are the things that God hates, they are pretty much self-explanatory, and I will not attempt to put my interpretations unto them. Use the concordance section in the Bible or a dictionary and look up the meaning of words you do not understand. Take God's words for what they are and not what you think they might be. I am a being like you. I surely do not understand everything that is written in the Bible, but I am most definitely going to try and obey all God's words. For, "In the beginning was the Word and the Word was with God and the Word was God" (*John* 1:1). If you continue doing any of these seven things, to the *lake of fire* you shall go (*Revelation* 21:8).

I know sometimes it is hard to tell the difference between good and evil in these dreadful times that we are now living in. However, "Woe unto them that call evil good, and good evil; that put darkness for light and light for darkness ... " (*Isaiah* 5:20). Of all the things that the Lord hates, a wicked heart will allow one to do anything that is evil and sinful against the Lord. However, if we love the Lord and one another like Jesus commanded in *John* 15:17, we will not want to sin against Him or each other. " ... For [love] shall cover the multitude of sins" (1*st Peter* 4:8). Let us love more; let us love each other as God loves us. Love will soften the heart and make it pure through Jesus Christ. Love is the reason God used me to write this book. I love you dearly. I want you and me to get to heaven. Your soul being saved is more precious to me than money in my pocket. Why do I say this? I know that if I take care of God's business He will take care of my business. For God I will live and for God I will die. Please see my sacrifice for you and let it not go in vain. Reach out to Jesus as I try to reach out to you through Him. Somebody is reading right now and God is saying, "Come, come unto me, I want to feed you with the bread of life, come." Is that person you? Will you listen today? Will you go on the path of righteousness? What are you waiting for? My friend, only God has hope for you and me. Listen!

The first sin I will write about is the sin of *Fornication*. I know this is not a popular topic among men, but the truth must be told. My friends, the truth shall make you free (*John* 8:32). This is also one of the sins that the world tells us that is not evil. The world will make you feel that it is good to shack up and get to know your partner literally inside and out before getting married. Some people even say that if you have sex without being married or live together for a while; you are considered husband and wife. This is a lie from the pit of hell and there you shall make your bed for lying in the bed of fornication. Fornication is simply having sexual relations with another without being married. When one fornicates, one sins causing another to sin. There involves lust, hate, and anger, all because there is no true love. In most cases, as the world says, "One just wants to get busy with no strings attached." There is no love here. For if you truly love each other then you would love God enough not to sin against Him. " … For God is love" (1*st John* 4:8). Nevertheless, please know that I am not saying that anyone is perfect. We all make mistakes. If you slip up, do not continue therein. Stop, and with a contrite heart ask your Father in heaven to forgive you. He will see through your heart and forgive you (*Isaiah* 55:7).

Also, when people fornicate, demons are being shared between them. Why do I state this? Because, " … know ye not that he which is joined to a harlot is one body? For two, saith He, shall be one flesh" (1*st Corinthians* 6:16). Fornication is a very evil thing to do. " ... The body is not for fornication, but for the Lord, and the Lord for the body" (1*st Corinthians* 6: 13). You can tell a fornicator when you see one by the lust in the eyes. I know, because I used to be this way. I used to walk around with evil deeds in my heart and lust in my eyes. However, I have been delivered and you too can be delivered by the precious blood of Jesus. " ... God commendeth His love toward us, for while we were yet sinners, Christ died for us" (*Romans* 5:8). So, "flee fornication. Every sin that a man doeth is without the body; but he that committeth fornication sinneth against his own body" (1*st Corinthians* 6:18). What on earth does this mean? " ... Know ye not that your body is the temple of the Holy Ghost which is in you, which ye have of God, and ye are not your own? For ye are bought with a price: therefore glorify God in your body, and in your spirit, which are God's" (1*st Corinthians* 6:19–20). My brethren, your body is not your own. It is for God's purpose.

Our body is where He dwells. Our body is His temple. Therefore, we need to keep His temple neat, clean, and in order for His use only. In addition, you brothers and sisters out there who say that you are saved and sanctified; if you commit fornication, the Bible reads in 1*st Corinthians* 5:11, do not keep company with any brother that fornicates, with such a one do not eat. Women are men's main weakness. "For the lips of a strange woman drop as a honeycomb, and her mouth is smoother than oil; but her end is bitter as wormwood … her feet go down to death and her steps take hold on hell" (*Proverbs* 5:3–5). A woman's beauty and charm can easily lure men into lust and fornication. However, men, we need to be strong and wise. My fellow brothers, please wait on the Lord and run for your lives. Brothers, if she is not your wife, get up out of her bed. Sisters, if he is not your husband, get up! In the twinkling of an eye, in the midst of your sin, Jesus can crack the sky and that will be it for you (*1st Corinthians* 15:52). Live a righteous life and watch, for you know not when Jesus will come (*Mathew* 24:42). Do not slumber; walk on the narrow path. Again I say, take heed, you never know when He will come. My God, my God, do not be caught in His Hands (*Hebrews* 10:31). Please, do not let Him come in the midst of your sin. That dreadful day, my friend, will be your very last.

Brothers, " … it is not good for a man to touch a woman, nevertheless, to avoid fornication, let every man have his own wife, and let every woman have her own husband. Render benevolence unto each other. The wife hath not power over her own body, but the husband: and likewise also the husband hath no power of his own body, but the wife" (*1st Corinthians* 7:1–4). This makes a lot of sense to me, people. If I can reasonably have you when I want and you can reasonably have me when you want, then there will be no need to go elsewhere allowing the devil to tempt us. "Hey, brother man, your wife does not want to love you tonight, why don't you go and visit Sally in the alley? She is always ready to love you." "Hey sister girl, your husband does not want to love you tonight, why don't you go and visit Don at the pond? He sure is ready to love you." Do not give Lucifer any room to lead you into sin. Resist the devil. Give unto your husband yourself and husband, give unto your wife yourself. Take heed. "Do not deprive one another except with consent for a time, that you may give yourselves to fasting and prayer; and come together again so that Satan does not tempt you because of your lack of self-control" (*1st Corinthians* 7:5, nkjv). Does any of this make sense to you? If you have wisdom, you will listen to the Word of God.

"Marriage is honourable in all, and the bed undefiled: but whoremongers and adulterers God will judge" (*Hebrews* 13:4). Yes, it is true what Paul wrote in *1st Corinthians* 7:9, " ... it is better to marry than to burn." However, not every man is for every woman and not every woman is for every man. "Be ye not unequally yoked together with unbelievers: for what fellowship hath righteousness with unrighteousness? And what communion hath light with darkness" (*2nd Corinthians* 6:14)? My brothers and sisters, I know this is hard. Nevertheless, contemplate on it and assess the situation here. God hates divorce (*Malachi* 2:16, nkjv). Thus, seen as though marriage is supposed to be done once, you better do it right. If you have a spouse that does not want to pray, fast, and worship with you, then what good is the marriage unto God? You better get a spouse in the church that first and foremost loves God. If you love God then you will want to please Him and please each other. Many marriages fail because people are unequally yoked and in it for themselves. They forgot about God. A marriage is a lifetime bond between the two of you and God. Do it once and do it right. Be not unequally yoked, problems will arise. Once again, for your own sanity and happiness take heed. My brothers and sisters, wait on the Lord and pray for a good spouse. He will give one unto you. "Ask and it shall be given you ... For everyone that asketh receiveth ... " (*Matthew* 7:7–8). Jesus also said in *John* 14:14, " ... Ask anything in my name, I will do it." Pray and wait! Do not rush into marriage, for we all know that "haste makes waste." Flee from fornication! You will be better for it. Just trust in God.

Another sin that the world tells us is a good thing is the sin of *Homosexuality*. This is not right! God created man and woman for each other *(Mark* 10:6–8). He formed Adam first. He then saw that it was not good for man to live alone, thus He formed Eve, a woman from the rib of Adam (*Genesis* 2:22). God loves the person, but He hates the sin of homosexuality. We were not created to be with the same sex. Even nature tells us that. Two men or two women cannot produce an offspring. Also, some plants would never pollinate if a male plant of the same species were not available. Yes, some animals can reproduce asexually. That is how they were created for God's own purpose.

Homosexuality then, is having sexual relations with another person of the same sex. It is a learned behavior. In *Romans* 1:26–27, Paul states that homosexuality is a vile affection where a man and a woman change the natural use of the opposite sex, which is against nature. Men burned in their lust, one toward another; men with men working that which is unseemly. People, think about what you are doing before you follow through with it. Homosexuality is displeasing to God. Thus, "If a man also lie with mankind, as he lieth with womankind, both of them hath commiteth an abomination: they shall surely be put to death; their blood shall be upon them" (*Leviticus* 20:13). The same goes for a woman-to-woman relationship. People are even protesting in favor of Homosexuals to be allowed to legally marry. In consequence, like the demise of Sodom and Gomorrah so shall these places of homosexuality be destroyed by God Almighty. For in Sodom and Gomorrah, the men wanted to sleep with the male angels that came to visit Lot. The men in the city had no idea that these men were angels. They saw that they were new in town and they said unto Lot, "… Bring them … out to us that we may know them carnally" (*Genesis* 19:5, nkjv). I see in books where people wrote that the men of the city did not want to sleep with the angels. They thought they were spies and came to see why they were in town. However, if you read past *verse* 5 of the latter chapter then you will see that Lot offered the men of the city his daughters instead. Why would he offer his daughters if the men did not want to sleep with the male angels?

Now, because of evil in the hearts of the men in Sodom and Gomorrah, God said, " ... The cry of Sodom and Gomorrah is great and because their sin is very grievous; I will go down now and see [if it is true what they have done]" (*Genesis* 18:20–21). Thus, upon seeing that truth lied within all that had been cried unto Him about Sodom and Gomorrah, " ... the Lord rained upon Sodom and Gomorrah brimstone and fire from the Lord out of heaven; and He overthrew those cities, and all the inhabitants of the cities, and that which grew upon the ground" (*Genesis* 19:24–25). My people, the Lord changes not (*Malachi* 3:6). He rained on Sodom and Gomorrah because of their pride (*Ezekiel* 16:49–50), and them giving into vile affections. He is going to do it again. All cities, countries, places, and people that practice sodomy, harlotry, and whoredom are going to perish like Sodom and Gomorrah. You do not have to listen to me, but God is coming. Do not let Him catch you slipping or sleeping. Additionally, those of us trying to take God's matters into our own hands, woe unto you. " ... He that is without sin among you, let him cast the first stone ... " (*John* 8:7). It is not up to us to hate, chastise, ridicule, kill, or burn homosexuals, like they do in my home country of Jamaica, West Indies. Let God handle His business. We need to love and pray for each other.

Now, I am not saying that we should accept the behavior of homosexuality; I know that it is wrong and is the spirit of the devil. Please take into account the scripture below.

> ... The king shall do according to his will; and he shall exalt himself, and magnify himself above every god, and shall speak marvellous things against the God of gods, and shall prosper till the indignation be accomplished: for that that is determined shall be done. Neither shall he regard the God of his fathers, *nor the desire of women*, nor regard any god: for he shall magnify himself above all.
>
> (*Daniel* 11: 36–37)

If you read further in this scripture you will realize that the king the Bible reads about here is the antichrist, which is the devil. He has no desire for women, because he is a homosexual and is against God's creation. Friends, the devil is so bold, that there lie among us homosexual preachers. If there is anything that I know, I can tell you that this is not right in the eyes of God. Now, with all that is written, it is not for us to judge anyone. God can save homosexuals. Their life is not finished because Jesus is truly a merciful God. Pray, my friends, pray for each other that God will intervene in each of our lives. The Spirit of the Lord is here on earth and so is the spirit of the devil. "For we wrestle not against flesh and blood, but against principalities, against powers, against the rulers of the darkness of this world, against spiritual wickedness in high places" (*Ephesians* 6:12).

Parents, teachers are in high places. The next time you visit your child's school, please talk with his teacher. Know who is teaching and guiding your children. Please pay attention to what your child is being taught. If there is anything you can take from this paragraph, let it be this, "Be not deceived: evil communications corrupt good manners" (*1st Corinthians* 15:33). Be attentive, for there is evil in high places and you truly know not what your child is being taught. Please, "train up a child in the way he should go: and when he is old, he will not depart from it" (*Proverbs* 22:6). You better hear me. I am not here to discriminate, but what is wrong cannot be right. The borrower is servant to the lender (*Proverbs* 22:7). Teachers educate by sharing/lending their knowledge. Some even share more than they should and children are like sponges, they absorb everything. Hear me please, because what your children absorb may never be released. I will write more on evil and the devil in the next chapter. Homosexuality is a sin.

The next sin is of grave importance. This is the sin that most people overlook. This is the very sin that causes disobedience unto God. This is the sin of *Pride*. A proud person feels that he does not need God, for he already has all he needs in this world. When you are proud, you cannot be humble unto

God. The only way God can use us completely is if we humble ourselves. A person full of pride, will not bow before God or anyone, but the devil. "Woe unto them that are wise in their own eyes, and prudent in their own sight" (*Isaiah* 5:21)! My friends, "everyone that is proud in heart is an abomination to the Lord: though hand join in hand, he shall not go unpunished" (*Proverbs* 16:5). Be smart, friend. Be humble, because "Pride goeth before destruction, and a haughty spirit goeth before a fall" (*Proverbs* 16:18). Pride leads to your demise. Of all the wealthy people in the world, how many of them truly love God? It is hard to love God when you are wealthy. For when you are wealthy it is hard to be humble unless you love God first.

Great men in the Bible were wealthy: David, Abraham, Job, King Solomon, and more, but they loved God first. They were not perfect, but because of being humble they always went before God in prayer. You do not believe me? Read the *Books of Genesis, Job, Psalm,* and *Proverbs* to see how humble these great men were, even in the midst of their trouble. King Solomon went as far as writing, " … vanity of vanities; all is vanity" (*Ecclesiastes* 1:2). Plus, before Solomon even uttered these words, King David asked the Lord to turn [his] eyes away from beholding vanity (*Psalm* 119:37).

King David was very humble. He let us know that, "A little that a righteous man has is better than the riches of many wicked" (*Psalm* 37:16). I am not saying that everyone who is rich is evil, prideful, and have not humility. I am simply saying that riches and pride go hand in hand when you do not truly love the Lord. King Solomon said it best, "Riches profit not in the day of wrath: but righteousness delivereth from death" (*Proverbs* 11:4). Why am I writing all this? Simple, look at the world we are living in today. Look at all these actors, singers, sport icons, moguls, and all the people in the public eye. They marry and remarry like it is something fun to do. They are wealthy, they are proud, not humble, they are all about "I," they fornicate, they do drugs, they get drunk, they are "cool," they do evil, they have no respect for God, and they despise God and holiness. Yes, my friends, can you deny what I am writing? Well, sure you can, but is it the truth? By humility and fear of the Lord are **riches**, honor, and life (*Proverbs* 22:4). Better it is to be of a humble spirit with the lowly, than to divide the spoil with the proud (*Proverbs* 16:19). Jesus even told His disciples that, " ... Blessed be ye poor, for yours is the kingdom of God" (*Luke* 6:20). Also, the unkind rich man lifted up his eyes in hell and was in torments (Luke 16:23). In addition, " ... it is easier for a camel to go through a needle's eye, than for a rich man to enter into the kingdom of God" (*Luke* 18:25).

Can you see here what riches can do? My God, just think about the comparison made between a camel and a rich person who does not love God first. Now, what makes matters worse is that a common man like myself did not make this comparison, Jesus Himself made it. Riches will make you feel like you are bigger than God. In consequence, " … whosoever shall exalt himself shall be abased; and he that shall humble himself shall be exalted" (*Matthew* 23:12). Watch out! For like it is asked in *Matthew* 16:26, what does it profit to be blinded by sin while seeking for fame, gaining the whole world, and losing your soul? It profits nothing my friend. Your goal should not be to seek fame and money in this world, but to look to Jesus and try to make it into heaven. For in heaven, there is eternal life and happiness abounds. We are nothing but dust and our lives are but " … a vapour, that appeareth for a little time and then vanisheth away" (*James* 4:14). There is no amount of money in this world that can bribe God. Buy the truth and sell it not (*Proverbs* 23:23). "For the love of money is the root of all evil … " (1*st Timothy* 6:10).

Saints of the living God, we are not to walk around thinking that we are number one. This is why the devil got banished from heaven. The devil is puffed up with pride.

> How art thou fallen from heaven,
> O Lucifer, son of the morning!
> How art thou cut down to the
> ground, which didst weaken the
> nations! For thou hast said in
> thine heart, I will ascend into
> heaven, I will exalt my throne
> above the stars of God … I will
> ascend above the heights of the

> clouds; I will be like the most
> High.
>
> (*Isaiah* 14:12–14)

Be wise and careful not to get beside yourself, that you think you are greater than anyone else in this world, let alone God. Humble yourselves. Do not make the Lord humble you like he humbled King Nebuchadnezzar. Yes, a king. The king got beside himself as if he was the one that built himself and the great city of Babylon. Thus, God banished him to a forest, molded his body in the form of animals, and made him eat grass for seven years until he came to his senses, realizing that God has dominion over *all things* (*Daniel* 4:33–34). Be humble in the Lord. Most of the people seeking for fame think that they are unstoppable. The next time you listen to a rap song or a mogul speak, listen for the pride that cometh from their heart.

The next sin is one that a lot of people think is not a sin, but merely a way to get outside of yourself and have a good time. This is the sin of *Drunkenness*. This is the sin that will literally cause you to lose your mind and do anything that the devil wants of you. The Bible reads, "Be sober, be vigilant, for your adversary the devil, as a roaring lion, walketh about, seeking whom he may devour" (*1st Peter* 5:8). My brethren, do you see what the devil can cause you to do when you are out of your mind? How can you resist him if you do not even know where you are? I think us as a people give ourselves too much credit where sin is concerned. Do you really believe you want to hurt yourself? Do you truly believe that you want to get drunk to a stupor, waiting in the hospital for your stomach to be pumped? People, it is the devil. If he can get you to lose your mind, then he can take control. This is why God, through Peter tells us to be sober. "Woe unto them that rise up early in the morning, that they may follow strong drink; that continue until, night, till wine inflame them" (*Isaiah* 5:11)! Also, "Woe unto them that are mighty to drink wine, and men of strength to mingle strong drink" (*Isaiah* 5:22).

If you do not get it by now I am going to say it, " ... Be not drunk with wine, wherein is excess; but be filled with the Spirit" (*Ephesians* 5:18). I remember my days as a college Resident Assistant. College life comes with a lot of stress, pain, and torture of the brain. One has to be dedicated and willing to push in order to accomplish something beneficial. Most of my fellow students thought otherwise. They drank alcohol like there was no tomorrow. All they knew how to do was drink, party, and fornicate. I knew females that "slept" with different guys every weekend and would always be passed out afterwards. Gentlemen, this is rape. Parents have no idea what they send their children to school to learn. They think it is to get a good education but they are so very wrong. Their children get an education that is beyond this realm. They get an education from the devil, an education of how to lust and fornicate. I am not saying that college is of no value. College can be a great place to excel in the world. However, young men and women, who are not fully grounded, go to college and get whipped by the devil. Here is a little secret, if you have the mind to be messed up, then college is the place to be. In college you will find drug dealers, pimps, alcoholics, rapists, abusers, and many other forms of deviant spirits. In other words, if you are in college to have a good time, then you can be messed up if you want to be. I have lived it and I know what college can do to a young, wondering mind. All these deviant behaviors are stemmed around the consumption of alcohol, which is generally the idol of college students. Have you ever seen pictures of college students? There is always the beer pose or the beer pyramid to see who can pose the best next to their idol. Alcohol is always prevalent on college campuses. I also knew a few girls in college who "slept" with more than twenty men because of too much alcohol consumption.

You that are reading, this might apply to you or your daughter. My God, college life is not all it is said to be. I am truly afraid to send my children to college when I do have them. What I have seen over the years truly scared me. Yes, I fornicated, but it was always with someone I dated, not a "hook up" or a drunken buddy. I am in no way making excuses for myself either, but alcohol makes any situation ten to twenty times worse. Even in the very cold wintertime, you can see college females wearing skimpy outfits to parties like it is summertime. They do this because they are practicing whoredom and they do not even know it. They are trying their best to entice men who they wish to "hook up" with at the end of the night. Some do not even wait until the end of the night, because they seem to be in dire heat. I am truly sorry if this offends you, but I must keep it real. Be real! For it is the truth anyhow.

My fellow men, I am talking to you as well. Trying to put on your best outfits with some Cool Water cologne just because you want to meet that fine damsel to take advantage of when she is drunk. Yes you do, I have seen it with my very own eyes. Then before the night is even out, you find two or three more drunk damsels to "lie" with. Men are so very evil. This is not new though. The devil has been robbing people of their mind with wine for years. "Whoredom and wine and new wine take away the heart" (*Hosea* 4:11). Wine and sex goes hand in hand and allows one to just flow into fornication (*Hosea* 4:18). Sometimes people do not even remember what happened the night before. This is scary, friend; this is how you get viruses. The AIDS virus stays dormant for years. So men and women, today, you might be a walking virus. You better repent, pray, and hope that God has mercy on you. For "wine is a mocker, strong drink is raging: and whosoever is deceived thereby is not wise" (*Proverbs* 20:1). My people, can it be written any clearer? Why do you drink something that is going to kill you and take you out of the plan of God? I pray that you will take heed and take hold of your body, which is the temple of God.

The next sin is the mother of them all. Why? The *sin of Disobedience* will allow you to go against any and everything that is like God. You do not want anything to do with what is God-like. You become rebellious, puffed up with pride, drink alcohol, and fornicate with men, women, same sex, or beasts of any kind. Yes friend, when you are disobedient you will allow the devil to take control of you and do with you as he desires. His goal, my friend is to kill you before God reaches you. Believe me though, friend, God has been trying to reach out to you, because it is not His will to see any man perish (*2nd Peter* 3:9). However, because of your disobedience, the devil is going to kill you. Be wise, brethren. Be wise!

I will write about women first. "I will therefore that men pray everywhere, lifting up holy hands, without wrath and doubting. In like manner also, that women adorn themselves in modest apparel, with shamefacedness and sobriety; not with [braided] hair, or gold, or pearls, or costly array; but (which becometh women professing godliness) with good works" (*1st Timothy* 2:8–10). How many women in the church today wear jewelry and have their hair braided? Let me continue with the disobedience of women. How many women go to church with their head uncovered? " ... Every woman that prayeth or prophesieth with her head uncovered dishonoreth her head: for that is even all one as if she were shaven. For if the woman be not covered, let her also be shorn: but if it be a shame for a woman to be shorn or shaven, let her be covered" (*1st Corinthians* 11:5–6).

Ladies, for the love of God, please cover your head in the sanctuary and when you pray.

In addition to the disobedience of women, there are many females today that believe they do not have to be in subjection to a true husband. This is ungodly and disobedient. The Bible reads, " ... the man is not of the woman; but the woman of the man. Neither was the man created for the woman; but the woman for the man ... " (1*st Corinthians* 11:8–9). Furthermore, just as the Bible reads that a woman should be in subjection to her husband in a marriage (1*st Peter* 3:1), a woman should also be in subjection to the male/pastor from the pulpit. A woman should not be preaching. Paul clearly said, "Let the woman learn in silence with all subjection ... *I suffer not a woman to teach, nor to usurp authority over a man*, but to be in silence" (1*st Timothy* 2:11–12). There are a lot of heartaches that comes with preaching and teaching the gospel. Preaching is a very high and intense calling. Women should not have to bear the anguish and pain the apostles bore for preaching about the gospel and holy living. Listen to Apostle Paul: women should not be in charge of the pulpit. It has never been this way and it is not how God intended for things to be. All Jesus's disciples were males. There has to be a reason for this. Namely the reasons written above, the pain, torture, torment, and sufferings that come along with preaching truth.

Do not think I am being sexist in any way, shape, or form. I know that man made laws, whether hidden or open that make it hard for women to feel they are of value and worth. But these are men, not God. It is because of His love why you are being protected from the hardships of preaching the gospel. The Lord knows all things. Trust in Him. Yes, Apostle Paul wrote these words. But, he wrote them under the unction of God. Trust in God's Word. He knows all. Now ladies, if you want to do otherwise, this is completely on your own terms. However, you are outside of the Word of God if you preach. Sisters, you better hear me, " ... I would have you know, that the head of every man is Christ; and the head of the woman is man; and the head of Christ is God" (1*st Corinthians* 11:3). Again I write, women should not be in charge of the pulpit or the church. Do not be disobedient.

Now that we have discussed the pulpit issue, let us continue on the topic of obedience in marriage. Wives, please be obedient to God and your husband. You are not doing it for the man only; you are doing it first and foremost because you love God. Please do not forget when Adam was in the Garden of Eden, God saw that it was not good for man to live alone so he created Eve from one of Adam's ribs. Thus, " ... wives, be in subjection to your own husbands; that, if any obey not the word, they also may without the word be won by the [conduct] of the wives ..." (1*st Peter* 3:1*).* Here, the importance of your obedience is shown. You being in subjection can allow a wandering husband to turn back to God. It is very important that you obey the Word. Also, when you garnish yourselves:

... Let it not be that outward
adorning of plaiting the hair,
and of wearing of gold, or of
putting on of apparel; But let it
be the hidden man of the heart,
in that which is not corruptible,
even the ornament of a meek and
quiet spirit, which is in the sight
of God of great price. For after
this manner in the old time the
holy women also, who trusted in
God, adorned themselves, being
in subjection unto their own
husbands: Even as Sara obeyed
Abraham, calling him Lord ...

(1*st Peter* 3:3–6)

If you are a woman that wears jewelry and
make-up, you have the spirit of a harlot, and a harlot
is not pleasing to God.

Wherefore, O harlot, hear the
word of the lord: Thus saith
the Lord GOD, Because thy
filthiness was poured out, and thy
nakedness discovered through
thy whoredoms with thy lovers,
and with all the idols of thy
abominations, and by the blood
of thy children, which thou didst
give unto them; Behold, therefore

I will gather all thy lovers, with whom thou hast taken pleasure, and all them that thou hast loved, with all them that thou hast hated; I will even gather them round about against thee, and will discover thy nakedness unto them, that they may see all thy nakedness. And I will judge thee, as women that break wedlock and shed blood are judged; and I will give thee blood in fury and jealousy. And I will also give thee into their hand … And they shall strip thee also of thy clothes, and shall take thy *fair jewels*, and leave thee naked and bare.

(*Ezekiel* 16: 35–39)

Silver and gold were things offered up to idols (*Exodus* 20:23). Silver and gold are also the idols of the heathen; the work of men's hands (*Psalm* 135:15). Apostle Paul asked, " … what agreement hath the temple of God with idols? For ye are the temple of the living God … " (*2nd Corinthians* 6:16). Our bodies are the temple of God, let not silver and gold be found on our members, unless it is a ring, which symbolizes marriage. Ladies, you do not need these things that you think make you look fine. It is better to obey than repenting or suffering the consequences (*1st Samuel* 15:22). King David even stated that, the law of God's mouth is better unto him than any silver or gold (*Psalm* 119:72). Please, do not worry about the splendor of the flesh, for God takes pleasure in our natural state. " … He will beautify the meek with salvation" (*Psalm* 149:4).

In continuance, *Deuteronomy* 22:5 reads, "The woman shall not wear that which pertaineth unto a man, neither shall a man put on a woman's garment: for all that do so are abomination unto the Lord thy God." The desire to be like men in attire has far long affected the true characteristics of womanhood. Sometimes it is even hard to tell if a person is male or female, it ought not to be so. A female should not wear pants. Not only do females wear pants, the pants they wear are so tight that it squeezes in the shape of the body and magnify everything that God has given unto them. This makes things difficult for us men. It is sometimes truly hard when men are on the street and a female is in front walking and shaking her buttocks. Yes, females do that. The attention given unto a woman that wears tight clothing is nothing but lustful attention. This causes a man to lust in his heart. God said in *Matthew* 5:28 *that*, if you lust in your heart, then you are committing a sin. Friends, from the heart comes evil deeds (*Jeremiah* 17:9). "Wherefore God also gave [man] up to uncleanness through the lusts of their own hearts, to dishonour their own bodies between themselves" (*Romans* 1:24).

Ladies, yes a man should be responsible and wise. However, why do you tempt us? Why do you wear such tight clothing, that sometimes when you eat you have to unbutton? Why do you wear such tight clothing that you have to jump on the bed, squat on the floor, and whatever else you have to do in order to get it on your body? This is very wrong in the eyes of God. Thus, any woman that tempts a man, causing him to sin in his heart is an evil woman. You have a likened spirit to that of a harlot and the queen of all harlots, Jezebel. Read 1*st Kings chapters* 16 *to* 21 to learn more about Queen Jezebel. You do not want to be like this woman. A nice skirt or dress that fits well, keeps the body modest and orderly. A pant plunges your buttocks out and makes it look very appealing to the lustful and not so lustful eyes. Now, a woman can be just as immodest in a dress also. Please wear one that fits well.

Let me share an incident with you. One day I was in church getting my praise on. Three sisters then sat down in front of me wearing skirts, but they were very tight. I was looking to Jesus and worshipping Him, but my eyes wandered as all three of them stood up to get their praise on. Good God from glory, I had to run to the other side of the room. I had to scamper away from seeing what I should not have to see in the church. Here I am in the church and it felt like I was still on the streets. Please ladies, do not tempt us, please. Wear a dress that fits well and blouses that cover your cleavage. Brothers, you also, wear pants that fit and shirts that are loose. Stop wearing tight clothing to church or anywhere where females or people in general can see your body plunging out. Not only is it wrong, it also does not look pleasant.

Nevertheless, with all that has been written, I know some will still say that a man should be responsible for his own eyes and that the customs of time has changed through the age of grace and not being under the Mosaic Laws any longer. However, the issue of not wearing what pertains to the other sex deals with the morality and the nature of God. A woman should in no way, shape, or form look like a man. Peter used Sarah as an example of how women ought to be (1st *Peter* 3:6). Even men in Scotland that wear kilts, yes it is a part of their culture, but a man should not be wearing skirts. This is in the Word, not my words.

Anyhow, let me continue with my brothers. Just like women, men ought not to wear jewelry, make-up, and all these things. Where it concerns the head of a man, when ye pray, " ... a man indeed ought not to cover his head, forasmuch as he is the image and glory of God: but the woman is the glory of the man" (1st *Corinthians* 11:7). Also, my brothers with long hair, braids, and twists, these are abominations unto the Lord. "Doth not even nature itself teach you, that, if a man have long hair, it is a shame unto him? But if a woman has long hair, it is a glory to her: for her hair is given her for a covering. But if any man seem to be contentious, we have no such custom, neither the churches of God. Now in this that I declare unto you I praise you not ... " (1st *Corinthians* 11:14–17). Before I move on, from this very Bible verse it shows that a female should not cut her hair, because her hair is her glory and it has been given to her for a covering. This is the Word of God, not mine.

Now, men, let's talk about how to treat your wives. Not because she is in subjection of you, means that you should abuse or think that she is beneath you. She is surely not beneath you. The Bible reads, you should "[submit] yourselves one to another in the fear of God" (*Ephesians* 5:21). This clearly shows that you need to work together. Not because she is your wife and you are the head of the household means that she is your footstool. You love yourself, right? You would not do anything to harm your very body, unless you are possessed with something! "So ought men to love their wives as their own bodies. He that loveth his wife loveth himself. For no man ever yet hated his own flesh; but nourisheth and cherisheth it, even as the Lord the church" (*Ephesians* 5:28–29*)*. Treat her with respect and love, my brothers, and she will do anything for you. A woman is very loyal and if you do right by her, she will do right by you, stick with you, and most of all, obey you, if she is not contentious (Proverbs 21:9 and 19). You do not believe me? Try it today. Make every effort to respect and truly love a woman and you will see.

OK, I cannot end this portion of this chapter without talking about piercing. Men and women, nose rings, ear rings, toe rings, excessive rings, necklaces, and bracelets, all these things are not of God. Piercing, markings/tattoos, and cutting of the flesh are wrong (*Leviticus* 19:28). Man should leave his body in its natural state, because it is the temple of God. You should not put things offered up to idols on the temple of God. Do you get it now? Your body is where God lives, treat it with respect, treat His home nicely. Be holy unto the Lord thy God.

In consequence, " … if any man that is called a brother be a fornicator, or covetous, or an *idolater*, or a railer, or a drunkard, or an extortioner; with such an one no not to eat" (1*st Corinthians* 5:11). "For this ye know, that no whoremonger, nor unclean person, nor covetous man, who is an *idolater*, hath any inheritance in the kingdom of Christ and of God. Let no man deceive you with vain words: for because of these things cometh the wrath of God upon the children of disobedience" (*Ephesians* 5:5–6). My friends, I need not explain anything here; the Lord will speak and has spoken for Himself. Brethren, I know that I am no one special. I am not even a theologian or a pastor. I even consider myself to truly be the least of all my church brothers. Plus, I am only 27 years of age. What could God want with me? I will write this, God is not a respecter of persons (*Romans* 2:11), and I am so very delighted that he chose me to write to you. All God is looking for is a vessel that will be obedient, not vain in thoughts or deeds, and can be used for His glory. Please read *Matthew* 11:25, and assess the latter written statement. Jesus, my Father up above, I give you all the honor, all the praises, and all the glory. To you, I give my all. Amen! I am just a vessel He is using to bring you out of darkness into the light of His Word.

I truly thank you for taking the time to read thus far. My only hope is that you take heed and listen to what He is saying to you. For these are not my words, but the Word of the Ever Living and Most High God.

> Therefore whosoever heareth these sayings of mine, and *doeth them*, I will liken him unto a wise man, which built his house upon a rock: And the rain descended, and the floods came, and the winds blew, and beat upon that house; and it fell not: for it was founded upon a rock. And every one that heareth these sayings of mine, and *doeth them not*, shall be likened unto a foolish man, which built his house upon the sand: And the rain descended, and the floods came, and the winds blew, and beat upon that house; and it fell: and great was the fall of it.
>
> (*Matthew* 7:24–27)

Be obedient to the Word of God.

THE SIDE EFFECT
OF SIN

The side effect of sin is death *(Romans 6:23)*. If you have not repented of your sins and perpetually continue in your carnal ways, you are going to die! For this reason, " ... hell hath enlarged herself, and opened her mouth without measure ... and [you who continue in your carnal ways] shall descend into it" *(Isaiah 5:14)*. The Lord thy God sits on high and looks down low, beholding both the good and evil *(Proverbs 15:3)*. He also makes the sun rise on both the good and the evil and sends rain on both the just and the unjust *(Matthew 5:45)*. To Him it is always daylight. He sees all you do both in the dark and light *(Psalm 139:11–12)*. Thus, not because you are healthy and wealthy means you are blessed. The price you pay for sinning is death. Wake up! Amen.

THE REDEMPTION OF SIN

"For all have sinned and come short of the glory of God" (*Romans* 3:23). Thus, without the shedding of Jesus's blood, there would be no redemption of sins (*Hebrews* 9:22). "Therefore, if any man be in Christ he is a new creature: old things have passed away; behold, all things are become new" (*2nd Corinthians* 5:17). To be saved, one must first *repent* of one's sins, be baptized in the name of the Lord Jesus Christ, and then the gift of the Holy Ghost shall come with fire from above (*Acts* 2:38). Jesus is the name that saves. "Neither is there salvation in any other; for there is none other *Name* under heaven given among men where by we *Must* be *Saved*" (*Acts* 4:12). The Bible even reads about Jesus before He was born and what He was going to do. " ... She shall bring forth a son, and thou shalt call His name JESUS: for He shall save His people from their sins" (*Matthew* 1:21). You must get your baptism right, so that you can die right. Father, Son, and Holy Ghost cannot save you. Jesus is His name and He washed us in His own blood to redeem us (*Revelation* 1:5). Let us look closely on the

Bible scripture 1*st John* 5:8, "And there are three that bear witness in earth, the spirit, and the water, and the blood: and these three agree in one." Peter, told us to be baptized in the name of Jesus Christ, right? People, the water represents the blood of Jesus Christ, which washes our sins away and then the Spirit will come. Do you see how the water, the Blood, and the Spirit agree in one? They are all linked together through Jesus Christ. Friends, please, it cannot get any clearer than this. For your sins to be redeemed, you must be baptized in the blood of Jesus Christ. I was baptized in the Trinity and I felt no power to resist anything. I wanted to make sure that I know that I am saved. So, when I heard the gospel, which is about the death, burial, and resurrection of Jesus Christ through the power of the Holy Ghost, I had to get my baptism right. For I truly wanted to be saved. I got baptized twice and so can you. That is if you have done it in the Trinity. Get it right, my friends. Please, get it right for your own sake.

"For when we were yet without strength ... Christ died for the ungodly" (*Romans* 5:6). " ... God commendeth His love toward us, in that, while we were yet sinners, Christ died for us" (*Romans* 5:8). Remember, " ... God said, Behold, the man is become as one of us, to know good and evil: and now, lest he put forth his hand, and take also of the tree of life, and eat, and live forever" (*Genesis* 3:22). This scripture is letting us know that the tree of life will give one eternal life and that because they have sinned against God, Adam and Eve were not allowed to eat thereof. Now, *Romans* 5:15 tells us that sin came into the world because of one man, Adam. However, the gift by grace and of life also came into the world because of one man. That man is Jesus Christ and the gift of life is the Holy Ghost (*Romans* 5:15). Reach forth your hand, like God said way back in the *Book of Genesis*, grab hold of the Holy Ghost, live righteously, and live forever. The Holy Ghost, I must have Him, the Holy Ghost, you need Him, the Holy Ghost will quicken you and give you life, the Holy Ghost, I thank God I have Him. Do you have the Holy Ghost? Well, if you do not, reread chapter two of this very book to learn how to receive the Holy Ghost. You cannot just reach forth your mortal hand for the Holy Ghost to come upon you. In *Matthew* 5:6, Jesus said, "Blessed are they which do hunger and thirst after righteousness: for they shall be filled." You must yearn for the Holy Ghost; you have to truly want Him. I hope by now you see why you need to be immersed in the water in no other name but in the name of Jesus.

Now that you are truly saved, what do you need to do? "Stand fast therefore in the liberty wherewith Christ hath made us free, and be not entangled again with the yoke of bondage" (*Galatians* 5:1). Yeah, well how can I do this? "Put on the whole armour of God, that ye may be able to stand against the wiles of the devil" (*Ephesians* 6:11). That armor my friend is the Holy Ghost. The Holy Ghost is for everyone and He will give you what you need to stand. " ... Ye shall receive power, after that the Holy Ghost is come upon you ... " (*Acts* 1:8). The Holy Ghost will give you the strength you need to resist all that the devil throws your way, all manner of evil. Friends, the Holy Ghost will keep you if you want to be kept. Yes, you can still have the Holy Ghost and sin. Why? The love of your flesh will cause you to do anything. That is why the Word of God told us not to be entangled again with the yoke of bondage. Stay away from both evil deeds and evil people. For, "blessed is the man that walketh not in the counsel of the ungodly nor standeth in the way of sinners, nor sitteth in the seat of the scornful" (*Psalm* 1:1). " ... Righteousness delivereth from death" (*Proverbs* 10:2)! Stay free my friends; stay free.

How else can you stay free from sin? By fasting and praying. Like my pastor always say, "If you fast, you will last and if you pray, you will stay." I will add to that by saying, "If you pray, you will not stray." Satan accuses us before God day and night (*Revelation* 12:10). So when we sin, it is a slap to God's face. He sent His only begotten Son to save us (*John* 3:16), and we allow the devil to successfully tempt us, then laughs in God's face. I honestly do not know about you, but I truly do not feel pleased about the devil laughing in God's face because of me. Tell the devil to get behind you. Fasting and praying keeps the flesh under subjection. Remember, man shall not live by bread alone, but by every word that comes from the mouth of God (*Deuteronomy* 8:3). Apostle Paul stated, " ... I die daily" (*1st Corinthians* 15:31). He disciplined and kept his flesh under subjection daily. Friends, you must fast sometimes, pray always (1*st Thessalonians* 5:17), and read your Bible daily to ward off the influences of the enemy. I will talk more about putting the flesh under subjection in the next chapter. All I will say, is that the devil hates people that pray. He cannot do anything to you that the Lord does not allow (*Job* 1:12). Job was a prayer warrior who was also a righteous man. Satan was allowed by God to destroy all of Job's possessions but he could not touch Job because God said, "No!" Thus, when Satan tempts you, if you hit your knees and truly pray, he has no choice but to flee from you. " … The effectual fervent prayer of a righteous man [avails] much (*James* 5:16). Pray, people. God said, "If my people which are called by my name, shall humble themselves, and pray, and seek my face, and turn from their wicked ways; then will I hear from heaven, and will forgive their sin … " (2*nd Chronicles* 7:14). Prayers are very powerful. Man should always pray and never faint (*Luke* 18:1). Remember, we have our own free will. Thus, if we do not pray and ask for a divine intervention in our lives from God, then He cannot intervene. If He intervenes without your will, then that is not free will. Pray always in the name of Jesus, for God's will to be done in your life.

How does one pray? I know it can be hard at times. However, start by hitting your knees and say, "Help Lord! Lord, you know all things, deliver me and draw me closer to you. I need a personal relationship with you, for I want to *reach heaven*." In addition, focus on all that God has done for you then just say, "Thank you for waking me this morning. Thank you for keeping me throughout this day. Lord, I just want to thank you for the activities of all my limbs." This is all it takes to jump start you in prayer then you will flow from there. You must also tell Jesus how much you love and adore Him. Plus, how much you are glad that He is in your life. Praise Him and then thank Him again, because God Himself stated, "Giving thanks is the sacrifice that honors me ... " (*Psalm* 50:23, tev). It is also best to pray with others. For Jesus said, " ... Where two or three are gathered together in my name, there am I in the midst of them" (*Matthew* 18:20). Thus, if you want a true blessing from God, pray with others and invite Him in your midst. At the end your prayer, put the stamp of Jesus on it. Always end your prayer with, "In Jesus's name I pray, Amen" (*John* 16:23 *and Colossians* 3:17).

As for fasting, start by not eating for about 5 hours, then 7, then 9, and so on. At my church, we have 6 a.m. prayer in the sanctuary every weekday morning. In addition to 6 a.m. prayer, Wednesdays are our day of fasting from midnight to about 4 or 5 p.m. This is about 17 hours of fasting and praying. You may drink water if you are thirsty, but that is about it. We keep the fast going at work also and pray when we get a spare minute. When you fast, pray and tell God the things that you want to fast for. Maybe it is for a friend to be saved, or for a new job. This is all between you and Jesus. Therefore, when you fast and pray, do it in secret that God can bless you openly

(*Matthew* 6:6 *and* 6:17–18). I fast on other days as well, for personal reasons. Stretch out, reach out to God beyond what the church orders and God shall surely see thy faith and bless thee. Faith, my friends, is a great thing, but " ... faith without works is dead" (*James* 2:20). " ... By works a man is justified, and not by faith only (*James* 2:24). We must do our part. We must do something. We must prove our faith. We cannot prove our faith to God by just sitting and doing nothing. *Reach* out to God by faith today. With all that I wrote above, you can no longer say, "I do not know how to fast and pray." Please read *Matthew chapter* 6 in its entirety to get a better understanding of fasting and praying. These are key to your success in sustaining until Jesus comes. I dare say fasting and praying are the two most important tools in your walk with Christ. They keep you in tuned with God. Praise Him!

In ending this chapter, I will state this: "If you repent of all your sins to God, get your baptism right, receive the Holy Ghost, become obedient, humble yourself, and live a clean and holy life; then my friend, you will be all set to make it to heaven." Early will I seek thy face and late shall I rise to praise thee. I shall always praise the Lord. My life has to be centered around Jesus Christ. I cannot and will not put Him on the back burner of the stove. This world will tell you that in order to be successful, you must have riches and a great education behind you. However, my friend, I am here to tell you that this is not so. For if you have all the riches of the world and have not Jesus as your first love, then you have nothing. Remember, this life is temporary and only the things that you do for Christ will remain. Anything you do without Jesus will eventually fail. Be wise, love the Lord thy God first, even above yourself. This is what it takes to be freed from your sins. I fell in love with Jesus. For in His arms I feel sheltered and in His arms I am never detached. Falling in love with Him is the best thing that I have ever done. I love you, Messiah. People, love the Lord thy God and give Him 100 percent of your life because 99 and ½ percent will not get you into heaven. Be righteous and holy unto God. "I have been young, and now I am old; yet have I not seen the righteous forsaken, nor his seed begging bread" (*Psalm* 37:25). If it had not been for the Lord on my side, tell me where would I be? Please tell me, where would I be? For I truly do not know. God bless you all. Be freed, from sin!

4.

Three enemies of God (the world, the flesh, and the devil)

THE WORLD AND THE FLESH

The world and the flesh cannot be separated because of sin. It is impossible for them to be separated because people make the world what it is today. What is the flesh? It is the physical nature of mankind, while the world is the earth and all that lie thereon. We are living in a very sin sick world today. People are plastic, which are dead on the inside and bogus on the outside. Their hearts are very far from God. People are trying to be good in the eyes of other people and not in the eyes of God. God wants real people to testify about Him. My fellow Christians, we are in the world, but not of the world (*John* 17:16). God has always called for there to be a separation between the church and the world. Brothers and sisters, to be the world's friend means to be God's enemy (*James* 4:4). So come out from among them and be ye separate (*2nd Corinthians* 6:17). We cannot serve God on a whole with this sinful body. Thus, as stated before, Paul said, " ... I die daily" (*1st Corinthians* 15:31). He placed his flesh under subjection in order to carry out the will of God. For, " ... they that are in the flesh cannot please God" (*Romans* 8:8). In addition, " ... they which are the children of the flesh, are not the children of God ... " (*Romans* 9:8). Remember, God is a Spirit and we must worship Him in spirit and not in the flesh. You need that Holy Ghost's spiritual power to truly worship the Lord and to place the flesh under subjection. Furthermore, your mind controls your flesh and if your mind is consecrated unto God then your flesh cannot carry out sinful deeds. "Love not the world, neither the things that are in the world. If any man love the world, then the love of the Father is not in him" (1*st John* 2:15).

The flesh is enticed by the things of this world. The flesh is against all the things of the Spirit, because the flesh wants what the flesh wants (*Galatians* 5:17). In this world you will find glamour, glitter, riches, vanity, and fame. These are the things that the flesh aspires to attain. However, in trying to attain these things, the farther you will stray from the hands of God. This is the reason Paul said, "I beseech you therefore, brethren, by the mercies of God, that ye present your bodies a living sacrifice, holy, acceptable unto God, which is your reasonable service. And be not conformed to this world: but be ye transformed by the renewing of your mind, that ye may prove what is that good, and acceptable, and perfect, will of God" (*Romans* 12:1–2). My God, do you see what Paul wrote? Our only job in this world is to serve God. It is our service. This world will take your mind off the things of God. Love not this world! Let me tell you something, "There is a way that seemeth right unto a man; but the end thereof are the ways of death" (*Proverbs* 16:25). Trust neither the world nor your own understanding. " ... For wide is the gate, and broad is the way, that leadeth to destruction, and many there be which go in ... because strait is the gate, and narrow is the way, which leadeth unto life, and few there be that find it" (*Matthew* 7:13–14). Broad is the way that leads to destruction. How many people do you know that live on Broadway? The next time you watch your television, check out your favorite actors, actresses, and singers. They all love Broadway. New York City has a Broadway. You cannot tell me that the name was not given as a result of the Bible. What about Las Vegas? Is it not called "Sin City?"

Do we still want to go on an expedition to these places? I dare say, "yes." How come? Because the flesh wants what is on Broadway. The flesh wants the glamour life. Broadway is not the way to heaven, my friends. Broadway leads to your demise. On Broadway, you can find the glamour lifestyle. The fleshly mind or man in his carnal state loves glitter and glamour. The entertainment industry is on Broadway. The devil lives on Broadway. So go on. Have fun on Broadway; my nemesis the devil shall meet you there. If you want eternal life, "enter ye in at the strait gate ... " (*Matthew* 7:13). This is the only and right way to paradise, with Jesus. You do not have to take my word for it; you do not even have to listen to me. My goal here is to help you get to heaven. Plus, remember, these are not my words.

These words are in the Bible. There is only one way to God (*John* 14:6). Thus, "Beware of false prophets, which come to you in sheep's clothing, but inwardly they are ravening wolves" (*Matthew* 7:15). If you believe that false prophet is I, then my friend, you are not wise.

So my friends, which road are you traveling today? The choice is yours. The entertainment industry is the biggest influence on human beings. First it was rock music, where artists used to kill animals and offer up their blood as a sacrifice at concerts. These sacrifices were not done unto God so they must have been done unto the devil. It is also evident that rock music was demonically influenced by the lyrics that came from these artists repertoire. I need not say these lyrics because we all who have heard a few rock songs from back in the 60's and so on know what these artists used to sing about. Now, the devil is taking over Hip hop because He noticed that minorities are now rising on the "cool side." Hip hop is the way of the minority culture and all they sing about are the struggles of life in the form of violence. These artists can tell you how to kill your mama, sell drugs, take drugs, degrade women, beat your wife, disrespect God, and get away with it all because it is entertainment and entertainment is cool. Well, it is not so cool now when we have all these gangs running around town shooting, raping, and killing each other as a result of the Hip hop culture. You see, the devil was a musical genius. God gave him this talent. He was Lucifer, son of the morning (*Isaiah* 14:12), who walked around with a [trumpet] in his body (*Ezekiel* 28:13). When he fell from heaven, he came to earth with all the power that God had given him. Lucifer's goal is to use his entire God-given power against God and God's saints. He wants to deceive the world from the hands of God (*Revelation* 12:9). I will talk more about old Lucifer later.

Sensuality or things of sexual nature is another big problem. Why? Sex sells. It all boils down to riches. Man will sell his soul to be rich. Plus, the reason sex sells is because the flesh is vivaciously enticed by sex. Man figured this out and in order to make lots of money, man uses what is best, sex. Sensuality appeals to the fleshly nature of man. We now know that fleshly nature is a sinful nature because you cannot please God in the flesh. Mediums of sensuality are: television, cable, movies, magazines, news, radio, advertisements, billboards, books, comic books, videos, video games, and striptease clubs. My friends, no one is immune to the sexual nature of man, from the baby to the adult; just look back at the mediums above. Most mediums appeal to both adults and children. Parents, pay attention to what your children absorb, you may never get it out. I am not saying that sex is a bad thing when done the right way. We are sexual creatures. God made us this way. However, sex is intended for married people to be fruitful and multiply so that the earth can be blessed (*Genesis* 9:1). Anyhow, I think that the biggest medium of sexual nature today is music. When music gets in you it allows the mind to be pensive.

A pornographic video can be seen and there is not much left for your imagination. However, when you can only hear it, your other senses are heightened, and the imagination will run wild. Such types of music are Hip hop and Rhythm and Blues. Besides singing about violence, sex is the mainstream with these types of music. These types of music tell you it is OK to fornicate and lust all day long.

Nevertheless, to learn more about the lives that most of these Hip hop and R&B artists lead, see the DVD, "The Truth Behind Hip hop," by G. Craige Lewis. Also, see his website www.exministries.com. Mr. Lewis, you can thank me later, sir. God bless you and thank you for showing me the truth behind the lifestyle of Hip hop. I thank God for you, sir. You see, before I came to truly know the Lord, I was a DJ, and all I did was listen to rap, Hip hop, reggae, and R&B. All this music helped me to do was to fornicate. Now, I can honestly say that I am free of playing secular music and engaging in sexual immorality. Thanks be to God. Secular music adds no value whatsoever to your soul. It takes away every bit of holiness within you. Music can make you happy, sad, cruel, nice, callous, viscous, etc. Whatever mood you want to be in, there is music for that. Let me tell you a true story: One day my brother, Omar and I went to the store to purchase laundry detergent. Upon entering the store, we saw a Jamaican man outside selling music Cds, while blaring reggae music from his car. He then saw us and offered to sell us Cds. I exclaimed, "Jesus is the Way, my friend!" He replied, "Yeah, I know that.

I have gospel Cds as well, but if you want the devil, I can sell you him, too." I was in awe. However, he knew what he was saying. He was telling the truth. He wants to make money. If the devil is what the world wants, he is going to sell him to them in order to make his money. People need to be delivered. They know what is wrong, but they do it anyhow. Be wary about the type of music you pierce into your soul.

You cannot serve God and listen to "I want to lick, lick, lick you from your head to your toe," "I want to sex you up," "I have a wife, but I got two other girls pregnant," "I know we cannot have this relationship because of your husband and children, but what about me?" "If loving you is wrong, then I don't want to be right," and the mother of them all, "Secret lovers, that's what we are … we both belong to someone else, but we cannot let go, because what we feel, is all so real, so real." My God, what is this? What man in his right mind would want to hear these lyrics? Be holy! Be holy unto God. Praise Him, for it is your only duty. Love Him, and not the things of this world. In the mighty name of Jesus, be holy! " … Put ye on the Lord Jesus Christ, and make not provision for the flesh, to fulfill the lust thereof " (*Romans* 13:14). Saints, who have the Holy Ghost, " … we are the circumcision, which worship God in the spirit … and have no confidence in the flesh" (*Philippians* 3:3). Thus, be holy like your Father in heaven is holy. Jesus saved us. He saw us polluted in our own blood and said, " … Live … " (*Ezekiel* 16:6). He could have left us in our filth.

He could have passed us by, but he let us know that when He sees consecrated blood, He will pass over us (*Exodus* 12:23). In other words, if you are in Christ, and have been washed in His precious blood, you will also live in Christ. For without the shedding of His blood upon you, there will be no remission of your sins (*Hebrews* 9:22). Hence, whom the Son made free is free indeed (*John* 8:36). There is a lot to grab hold of in this paragraph. Pray and ask God for understanding. While praying for understanding, please be free and holy. The blood of Jesus Christ be upon you. Amen.

THE DEVIL

For those constant wandering minds that are curious about the devil's existence, you better believe it. He is as real as real can be and he is here on earth to torment us every second of every day (Mathew 4:1–11). Anyhow, everything that God made was good and perfect (Genesis 1:10), even Lucifer. What caused him to have that first evil thought? Why did he have prideful thoughts? So much pride that he thought that he could overthrow God. He then convinced a third of God's angels to join him (*Revelation* 12:4 *and* 9), and yet they were created perfectly by God, too. What happened? All I can say is, we all have free will. We have the will to do as we please for the most part. Some people think they can and should do as they wish. This is a spirit from the devil himself. Let me tell you a secret, the devil is nothing but a stupid spirit and all he needs is company. Will you give him company? Well, I used to, but not anymore. When you sin, you are in the company of the devil and are servant to him (*John* 8:34). Man, the devil was God's top angel (*Ezekiel* 28:14). He knows he cannot win against God. My friends, the devil knows God. He also knows that we have never seen God (*John* 1:18), and that we believe only by faith. Thus, if he can affect our faith in God, then he can cause us to stray away from God's plan. He wants as many of us to go to hell with him for he has already been defeated (*Revelation* 12:12). Trust me friends, he also knows that he has lost the battle and the war with God. Do not let him take you with him, do not let him make you doubt Jesus, do not let him tell you that baptism in Jesus's name is not necessary, do not let him tell you that you already have the Holy Ghost and that it is just a warm feeling, don't let him!

Saints and friends, here is a blatant example of the devil's plot against Jesus and His saints. In *Acts* 9:15, God told Ananias, a true man of His, that He was going to send Paul, the Apostle to preach His Word unto the Gentiles. Paul began preaching the Word of God throughout the *Book of Acts*, then wrote letters to the churches of the Corinthians, Galatians, Romans, Philippians, Thessalonians, and others. However, the churches of today are refusing to adhere to Paul's letters and teachings. Why? This is the work of the devil. Remember, his plan is to deceive the whole world (*Revelation* 12:9). Peter and Paul told the churches that we must be baptized in the name of Jesus to be saved. However, we think we know more than the apostles because Jesus said, "Go baptize in the name of the Father, Son, and Holy Ghost" (*Matthew* 28:19). Yes, Jesus spoke, but Paul and Peter who are true men of His, fulfilled His commandment. Do not be deceived by the evil one. Peter and Paul truly knew what Jesus wants us to do.

My friends, be wise, Satan walks the earth to and from, seeking whom he may deceive (*Job* 1:6–7). The devil was a murderer from the beginning of time, there is no truth in him; he is a liar and father of it (*John* 8:44). He wants to kill you before you get to Jesus. For if you die with your sins on you, not being washed in the blood of Jesus, then most likely you will be with the devil in the end. The devil wants you badly; he is working real hard to get you. Once again, this is not my word.

Why do you think a person would use a gun, knife, or any other weapon to harm another? Why do you think there are so many crimes in this world? Let me tell you, people with evil thoughts allow the devil to take residence within their soul and control of their flesh. So, because the sentence against an evil work is not executed speedily, it is fully set in the heart of men to do evil (*Ecclesiastes* 8:11). I tell you, it shall not be well with the wicked; his days shall be short (*Ecclesiastes* 8:13). My brethren, " … abhor that which is evil; cleave to that which is good" (*Romans* 12:9). Hence, "If it be possible, as much as lieth in you, *live peaceably* with all men" (*Romans* 12:18). Do not render evil for evil with anyone. For, " … God is angry with the wicked every day" (*Psalm* 7:11), and vengeance will be His (*Romans* 12:19). Do you want God to be angry with you? Do you want His wrath upon your head? My friends, you better listen and get it right with Him now! In consequence, when people do evil and find themselves against the ropes and feel miserable, sad, and empty inside, they start to search for answers. Well, I am here to tell you that the answer is in Jesus. There is no other way to salvation.

Again, Jesus is the Way, the Truth, and the Life. He will give you rest when you are heavy laden. He is a burden bearer. "For I know the thoughts that I think toward you, saith the Lord, thoughts of peace, and not of evil, to give you an expected end" (*Jeremiah* 29:11). "Trust in the Lord with all thine heart; and lean not unto thine own understanding. In all thy ways acknowledge Him, and He shall direct thy paths" (*Proverbs* 3:5-6). The devil does not want us to trust in the Lord. Resist the devil and he will flee from thee.

When the devil tempts you, go back to the scriptures and tell him, " ... get thee behind me, Satan: thou art an offense unto me: for thou [values] not the things that be of God, but those that be of man" (*Matthew* 16:23). I resist you today, old serpent. I rebuke you in the name of Jesus. You no longer have a place inside my heart. Jesus is my heart. You are a true example of one puffed up with pride. You had it all and blew it because of greed. I often pray in the precious name of Jesus that I will never even come close to being like you. Amen. My friends, Satan has only three tricks of the world. They are, the lust of the flesh, the lust of the eye, and the pride of life (*1st John* 2:16). Friends, the things that Satan has to offer are sweet, they look nice, and boy, do they feel real good. However, " ... the world passeth away, and the lust thereof: but he that doeth the will of God abideth forever" (*1st John* 2:17). So, if you want to live forever with Jesus, gird your loins with truth, put on the breastplate of righteousness, and prepare yourselves with the gospel of peace (*Ephesians* 6:14). "Above all, [take] the shield of faith, wherewith ye shall be able to quench all the fiery darts of the wicked ... take the helmet of salvation and the sword of the Spirit, which is the word of God: praying always with all prayer and supplication in the Spirit ... " (*Ephesians* 6:16–18).

Saints, this is a battle to the death with Satan. He " ... hath desired to have you, that he may sift you as wheat" (*Luke* 22:31).

Do not play with the devil, for he is not playing with us. He wants to destroy everything about you and me. But, who shall separate us from the love of Christ? For His sake we are killed frequently. Saints, we are accounted as sheep for the slaughter. However, in all these things we are more than conquerors through Christ that loves us (*Romans* 8:35–37). We can only overcome the devil through Christ, my friends. Thus, stay in the Word, live holy, and keep your mind on Jesus. For your own sake, come out of the world and put on the whole armor of God. We are going to need every bit of it to resist Satan and his demons of hell. The end time is near and Jesus is coming very soon. Stand for what is right, because in Jesus, " ... [you] might have peace. In the world [you] shall have tribulation: but be of good cheer; [He has] overcome the world" (*John* 16:33). Jesus already won, all we have to do my friends is live right and stand firm for what is of God until

He comes. Remember, "blessed are those who are persecuted for righteousness's sake: for theirs is the kingdom of heaven" (*Matthew* 5:10). Jesus continued by telling us to rejoice and be exceedingly glad for great is your reward in heaven. For the world persecuted the prophets before you and so shall you that are in Christ also be persecuted for His sake (*Matthew* 5:12). But, be not afraid of persecution or death. For Jesus already conquered death when he rose and walked out the tomb (*Romans* 6:9). Death is the fourth enemy of Jesus (1*st Corinthians* 15:26) and it no longer has dominion over Him (*Romans* 6:9). Just stand for righteousness at any cost, live holy, and trust in Christ if you want to make it to heaven. May God be with us all, in the mighty name of Jesus I pray, Amen.

5.

The second coming of Jesus Christ and the Bible

THE DEATH AND BURIAL OF JESUS CHRIST

Jesus came to earth to be an example for us. Jesus did not have to do the things He did in human form. He could have come down from heaven in His mighty glory. However, He came into this world as a baby via the womb of a woman, just like you and I. The only difference was that His birth was immaculately formed. His birth was not of the seed of man, but was conceived in Mary by the Holy Ghost (*Matthew* 1:20). Jesus came to earth to free us from sin, so that we may have life (*John* 10:10). My Jesus was slain by the sin of this world. He took on sin for us (*1st Peter* 2:24). He could have called legions of angels to destroy the world and set Himself free (*Mathew* 26:53), but His love toward us caused Him to suffer for us. He came to fight a battle that neither His angels nor us could withstand. The devil, my friends, is very powerful. "Woe to the inhabiters of the earth and of the sea! For the devil is come down unto you, having great wrath … he hath but a short time"

(*Revelation* 12:12). However, before Jesus bowed His head, He exclaimed, "It is finished" (*John* 19:30)! Jesus already won the war with Satan. The devil is trying to kill us to sway us from heaven. We can only sustain not by power or might, but by [God's] Spirit, (*Zechariah* 4:6). Get on your knees and pray. Pray for God's protection from the wiles of the devil. Pray! My Jesus died for me.

Now, my question is, would you give your life for someone who does not even know you? Would you give your life for a world that just does not want to live right? Would you die for me? I ask again, would you? My heart burns with pain when I think about all that Jesus did for me. My soul cries out to Him daily, and I thank God for saving me. Do you love Jesus? I love Jesus only because He first loved me. There is no greater love than the love of Jesus, because, Jesus is love.

THE RESURRECTION OF JESUS CHRIST

" ... Fear not; I am the first and the last: I am He that liveth, and was dead; and, behold, I am alive for evermore, Amen; and have the keys of hell and of death" (*Revelation* 1:17–18). Jesus rose from the dead (*Romans* 14:9 *and John* 20:14–16). Thus, the gospel was born. The gospel is the good news about the life, the death, the burial, and the resurrection of Jesus Christ (*1st Corinthians* 15:3–4). His resurrection brought about salvation through the Holy Ghost (*John* 20:22). Without salvation we would still be living in our sins under the Mosaic Laws. I would have been stoned to death by now. What about you? The gospel proclaims Jesus to be the only begotten Son of God (*John* 3:16) and God Himself, for in Him dwells all the fullness of the Godhead. " ... This gospel of the kingdom shall be preached in all the world for a witness unto all nations; and then shall the end come" (*Matthew* 24:14). Thank God for Jesus. Thank God for His grace and mercy. I have been washed by the blood through the resurrection of Jesus Christ. Jesus came from heaven to the earth, from the earth to the cross, from the cross to the grave and took the key of death from the devil, then ascended into heaven only to return again. This is the fullness of the gospel of Jesus Christ as we believe it and as it is written in the *Bible*. In addition to the gospel, there is the doctrine of Jesus Christ. The apostles, who were inspired by Jesus, wrote the doctrine. Some people say that the apostles are dead, but I say, "So what!" Jesus and His doctrine still lives on and you better believe it or you shall die in your sins (*John* 8:24) and be left behind when He comes back to judge His world. The doctrine consists of the teachings of Jesus Christ and you must be careful of anyone that " ... [causes] divisions and offenses contrary to the doctrine which ye have learned; and avoid them. For they that are such serve not the Lord Jesus Christ, but their own belly; and by good words and fair speeches deceive the hearts of the simple" (*Romans* 16:17–18). Are you simple at heart? Are you easily deceived? Grab a backbone and run with the doctrine of Jesus Christ! Amen.

Still do not want to believe in the doctrine of Jesus Christ? Well, because of your lack of faith, the devil has blinded you and caused you not to believe (*2nd Corinthians* 4:4). Thus, the gospel has been hidden from you because you are lost (*2nd Corinthians* 4:3). Friends, do not be misguided like the Orthodox Jews of old and new. They are still waiting for their Messiah, who, according to the 1997 *version of the Merriam-Webster's dictionary,* is the expected King, coming to save His people, the

Jews, from their enemies and restore Israel. They do not believe that Jesus is the Messiah, because of the nature of His birth and His poor up-bringing. A king is supposed to be rich. They thought the Messiah would come directly from heaven in His royal attire, not being born in a manger of an impoverished Mary (*Luke* 2:12). However, *Isaiah* 53:1–10 tells us that the Messiah was not going to be rich, comely, or be of desired beauty. The latter scripture also reads that He would bear our grief, be wounded for our sins, and be bruised for our iniquities. Was this not Jesus Christ (*John* 1:29)? Who came from heaven wrapped in swaddling clothes in a manger and was crucified on the cross for the sin of this wicked world? None other than Jesus Christ Himself. Jesus is in *Isaiah chapter* 53 and many other Old Testament scriptures, such as *Isaiah* 9:6, *Psalm* 8:4–5, *Psalm* 68:18, etc. How could the Jews know this if they do not have the New Testament about the gospel of Jesus Christ to make comparisons? The Bible reads that their minds are blinded by the veil of the Law of Moses from the Old Testament. That veil has been done away with through Jesus Christ (*2nd Corinthians* 3:14). Wake up, people! Jesus was and still is the Messiah. He came and left, only to return again. Why are you still waiting for His first coming?

Nevertheless, how else do I know that Jesus is the Messiah? *John* 4:25–26, when Jesus told the Samaritan woman at the well that He is the Messiah. Also, *John* 18:36, where Jesus declared Himself King when He said that His kingdom is not of this world.

Other applicable scriptures are *Matthew* 2:1–2, *Matthew* 28:18, *Luke* 2:8–38, *Luke* 4:16–22, *John* 6:14–15, and *Acts* 18:5. Saints and friends, Jesus is Lord and King over all things. He is the Anointed One. You better believe it and turn to Him. For only then will the veil that is covering your heart be removed (*2nd Corinthians* 3:15–16). The Holy Ghost, down in your soul will give you truth (*John* 16:13), remove that veil, and make you free (*2nd Corinthians* 3:17). This all goes back to chapter 2 of this very book that you are reading, on being saved by the power of the Holy Ghost. Thank you, Holy Ghost for helping me to link these scriptures together. No man has revealed these scriptures to me, but the Holy Ghost as I read the Word of God. Friends, ask Jesus to remove the gloomy veil from your heart today. For that veil remains today over the hearts of those who do not believe in the gospel of Jesus Christ. Thus, because of the Jews' unbelief and transgression, salvation has come to the Gentiles to make the Jews jealous (*Romans* 11:11). My fellow Gentiles, if you are not grateful for anything else in this world, you better be thankful that God turned to us because we are some wild people (*Romans* 11:17). Now, do not think for one second that you should speak against the Jews. For God will keep His covenant with them (*Deuteronomy* 7:12). The Lord never changes and He will destroy anyone who speaks against or interferes with the Jews and Israel (*Genesis* 12:2–3). Please, no matter what they do, do not speak against the Jews. Let them be for your own sake.

On a side note, the Jews from the bloodline of Abraham, Isaac, and Jacob are God's chosen people (*Romans 9:7 and Deuteronomy 7:6–7*). Thus, as can be read from these latter scriptures, the Arab nation from the seed of Ishmael are not God's chosen people. It all goes back as far as Sarah allowing Abraham to commit adultery with Hagar because of a lack of patience for God's promise of a son (*Genesis 16:2–4*). From Abraham, Hagar had Ishmael and Sarah had Isaac. God chose the seed of Isaac to be His people, because Ishmael was not in the plan of God (*Galatians 4:22–23*). Abraham cast out Ishmael, who went and started his own family in Arabia (*Galatians 4:24–25 and Genesis 21:20–21*), which follows the Islamic religion. Muslims consider Ishmael as their ancestor and a prophet [Qur'an 19:55]. A promise is a promise. God said that He would make a great nation out of the seed of Ishmael also (*Genesis 17:20–21*). Can anyone see the built up tension here? The reason that Muslims and Jews are fighting for rights to the holy land of Jerusalem today is because both Ishmael and Isaac are seed of Abraham. However, according to the Bible, all of Israel was promised to the seed of Jacob, whose name was later changed to Israel, who is also the seed of Isaac (*Genesis 13:14–15 and Genesis 35:9–12*). Jerusalem is the capital of Israel. Thus, as can be seen from latter scriptures, it belongs to the Jews. My friends, Jacob is Israel. The problem is Muslims do not believe in the Bible. So, they believe that Ishmael's seed has first rights to Jerusalem because Ishmael was Abraham's first born. This is all one big mess. Sin is a terrible thing. Abraham's sin is causing chaos between Muslims and Jews to this very day. Can you believe it? Now, do not think I speak against Abraham. He was a very holy and true man of God. No one is perfect. I used him here as an example because of what is going on today. To learn more, read upon the significance of the *Dome of the Rock* to see why Jerusalem is important to the Jews, Muslims, and Christians alike. Saints, "pray for the peace of Jerusalem … " (*Psalm* 122:6).

Friends, we are now living in the last days and the Messiah will be returning soon. Gentile or Jew, what will you do when He comes? Tell me; are you ready? If you should hear the trumpet sound right now, would you be in tears or would you jump for joy? Are you ready? Just stop and think for a little while, will He say, "Depart, I know you not" (*Luke* 13:27)? Or will He say, "Come, my good and faithful servant" (*Matthew* 25:21)? Are you ready? Do you think that all is well with your soul and spirit? Do you know? I ask again, are you ready? " … Have ye received the Holy Ghost since ye believed … (*Acts* 19:2)? Have you been washed in Jesus's name? Are you ready to meet the Savior? Are you headed on the right path? Have you been paying your tithes and offerings (*Malachi* 3:7–10)? Lastly, where is your final destination, heaven or hell? Do you know?

THE SECOND COMING OF JESUS CHRIST

Jesus lives and He is coming back to judge all! "The thief cometh not, but for to steal, and to kill, and to destroy: I am come that they might have life, and that they might have it more abundantly" (*John* 10:10). Additionally, when Jesus comes, " ... He shall reward every man according to his works" (*Matthew* 16:27). What are the signs of the coming of Christ? According to *Matthew* 24:6–15, these are the signs of the coming of Christ: There shall be wars and rumors of wars. Nations shall rise against nations. There shall be famines, pestilences, and earthquakes. Ye shall be hated and or killed for my name's sake. There shall be great tribulations. There shall arise many false witnesses. The love of many shall wax cold. Does it seem like the signs are already here? I feel the same way, my friend. We are living in the end times. There shall be the abomination of desolations. "For then shall be great tribulations, such as was not since the beginning of the world to this time, no, nor ever shall be" (*Matthew* 24:21). During all these signs, there will be many false prophets saying Christ is here. However, my friends do not be deceived by false Christs (*Matthew* 24:5). Jesus is not going to be here on earth talking to some guy down the street and you do not know it is He. Jesus is not coming to set His feet back on this earth. We that are Holy Ghost-filled will be caught up by the power of the Holy Ghost to meet Him in the air (1*st Thessalonians* 4:17). In addition, during the time of tribulations, no flesh shall be saved if those days are not shortened. However, Jesus told us that because of the elect few, the days of tribulations will be shortened and some will be saved.

> Immediately after the tribulations of those days shall the sun be darkened, and the moon shall not give her light, and the stars shall fall from heaven, and the powers of heaven shall be shaken: And then shall appear the sign of the Son of man in heaven: and then shall all the tribes of the earth mourn, and they shall see the Son of man coming in the clouds of heaven with power and great glory. And He shall send His angels with a great sound of a trumpet, and they shall gather together His elect from the four

winds, from one end of heaven to
the other.

(*Matthew* 24:29–31)

Again I ask: if you should hear the trumpet blow right now, will you be ready? " ... This generation shall not pass till all these things be fulfilled. Heaven and earth shall pass away, but my words shall not pass away" (*Matthew* 24:34–35). Will you be ready when Jesus comes? People, when Jesus comes, unless you can fly, if you do not have the Holy Ghost that I have, then you are going nowhere with Him. How can a dead soul without the life of the Holy Ghost's quickening power be caught up in the air to meet Jesus? You tell me, for I truly do not know. All I can say is, you better be in the number that are caught up in the air, for the day of the Lord will come as a thief in the night, and the earth and all therein shall be burned up (*2nd Peter* 3:10). However, when He comes, " ... shall He find faith on the earth" (*Luke* 18:8)? Will you be one of His faithful? If not, " ... who did hinder you that ye should not obey the truth" (*Galatians* 5:7)? Jesus is alive and He is coming. So, get your house in order and get ready to meet Him in the air. You see, I cannot fly, so I know I need the Holy Ghost's quickening power to raise my soul.

One person can make a difference, but it takes the courage, strength, and unity of others for the difference to make a change. My name is LeeRoy Uwain Bailey, Jr. I am saved, sanctified, Holy Ghost-filled, water baptized in Jesus's name, and I have found a new life in Christ. A sanctified, tongue talking, Bible reading, foot stomping, and hand clapping Pentecostal Apostolic Church is fire. Friends, I stand firm in the apostolic doctrine, which Jesus Christ Himself is, the chief cornerstone (*Ephesians* 2:20). I am a soldier in the army of the Lord; with my weapon being the Word of God. Friends, I love not the things of this world. For God I live and for God I will die. May God bless you and have mercy upon our soul. Please pray for me as I pray for you, in Jesus's name, Amen.

THE BIBLE

" ... The Word of God is quick, and powerful, and sharper than a two edged sword, piercing even to the dividing ... of soul and spirit, and of the joints and marrow, and is a discerner of thoughts and intents of the heart" (*Hebrews* 4:12). Take the Word for what it is and do not try to construe it in your own way. For, " ... no prophecy of the scripture is of any private interpretation" (*2nd Peter* 1:20). The Word is very powerful and will convict you into repentance. Let the Word in your heart. "For the prophecy came not in old time by the will of man: but holy men of God spake as they were moved by the Holy Ghost" (*2nd Peter* 1:21). Furthermore, all scriptures in the Bible are given by the inspiration of God and are profitable for doctrine, reproof, correction, and instruction in righteousness (*2nd Timothy* 3:16). Teach no other doctrine (*1st Timothy* 1:3), lest ye be cursed (*Galatians* 1:9). All that I have written came from the Bible. Thus, if you do not believe in the Bible, then this book will be of no value to you. Plus, if you do not believe in the Bible in its entirety, then you do not believe in Jesus because Jesus is " ... the Word of God" (*Revelation* 19:13). " ... Be ye doers of the

Word and not hearers only … for if any man be a hearer of the Word, and not a doer, he is like unto a man beholding his natural face in a glass" (*James* 1:22–23). Basically, you are not wise for following your own natural way, instead of the Word of God.

People, God made it clear that in comparison of the two, His Word is above His name (*Psalm* 138:2). This one is a brain buster, but follow me here. The name Jesus is a very powerful name. This name takes away sins (*Acts* 2:38). However, the word Jesus is the name of God, it identifies who He is. But, *the words in the Bible, are God* (*John* 1:1). Think about this, without the Word/Bible, you would not know about the power behind the name Jesus. You would not even know who Jesus is or what His name means. You would be praying to an unknown God (*Acts* 17:16–33). Please try not to be confused here. The Person named Jesus is God, but God Himself is more powerful than His name. God cannot be separated from His Word. You can call Him many names as reviewed in chapter two, but His Word is constant and unchanging. Thus, you better hold fast to God's words that are *in the Bible*. For His Word will not go back to Him void. Every word written in the Bible will come to pass (Isaiah 55:10–11). Friends, the Word of God is true. The Bible stands alone. God does not need us to interpret His Word. He will do it Himself. Jesus said, " … Blessed is ye that keepeth the prophecy of [the Bible]" (*Revelation* 22:7). The Bible is our manual. Every appliance we buy at the store comes with a manual, a guide on how to assemble your appliance or putting it together yourself. Well, this is the Bible with regards to our lives. You want to be inspired, read the *Book of Psalms*. You want wisdom, read the *Book of Proverbs*. How about a love story? Read the *Book of Songs of Solomon*. You want a sad story, read the *Book of Jeremiah*. A scary story, read the *Book of Revelation*. You want the Holy Ghost, read the *Book of Acts*. The Bible has all that we need. For healing, read the gospels, *Matthew, Mark, Luke, and John.*

Nevertheless, " … whatsoever things that were written … were written for our learning, that we through patience and comfort of the scriptures might have hope" (*Romans* 15:4). People in this world do wrong deeds because they do not know the scriptures (*Mark* 12:24). Take in the Word of Christ and be wise in the doctrine. For blessed is the man whose delight is in the law of the Lord and in His law doth he meditate day and night. He shall stand firm in Christ, never to be driven away. Please, feed your mind, body, and soul with the Word of God that you may live free and happy. " … For the joy of the Lord is your strength" (*Nehemiah* 8:10). The Bible is the way to Christ. How can you get to Christ without knowing how to get to Him? My friends, brothers, and sisters, the Bible is the key to the plan of salvation. Paul, the great apostle said, "For I am not ashamed of the gospel of Christ, for it is the power of God unto salvation to everyone that believeth … " (*Romans* 1:16). How do I truly know that the Bible is real? What do I have inside of me that keeps me believing in God's Word? The Holy Ghost. The Bible reads that I will quicken (*Romans* 8:11) and speak with other tongues (*Acts* 2:4) when I have the Holy Ghost within me. I am living this. I cannot deny the Holy Ghost. I have the Holy Ghost down in my soul just like the Bible reads. This is my comfort. Knowing that the Bible reads about something that I physically experience is a comfort to me. My experience with the Holy Ghost allows me to keep on believing that God and the Bible are real. How can I completely believe in anything without experiencing it? " ... no man can say that Jesus is the Lord, but by the Holy Ghost" (1*st Corinthians* 12:3). You need this Holy Ghost experience. He will show you that the Bible is for real. Please, read your Bible, pray always, and grow in Christ. May God ever add a blessing to the reading of His Word, in the mighty name of Jesus I pray, Amen!

6.

Interviews and excerpts: Four vital questions on obtaining eternal life

Key (year 2008):
Born-again Christian- John 3:5, *Acts* 2:38
Eternal life- 1*st John* 5:11–13
Holy Ghost- Acts 2:4, *Acts* 1:8, *Romans*
8:10–11, *and Romans* 8:26–27
How to be saved- Acts 2:38, *John* 3:5

Pastor Chambers

Background:

I am a black, American male Baptist preacher of a Baptist church in California. I am 54 years old and I have been a minister for 27 years and pastoring for 16 years.

Who do you consider a born-again Christian?

Any person who has repented as a believer in Jesus Christ and has made an open confession of that belief. Then has had a supernatural transformation by God (*Romans* 10: 9–10 *and John* 3:6).

What does eternal life mean to you?

It means life eternal with God, and a passing from death unto life, and having Jesus Christ as my Savior (1*st John* 5:11–13).

What is your experience with the Holy Ghost?

He, the (Holy Ghost) has done in my life what Jesus said He would do in the scriptures. He has been leading and guiding me into all manners of truth through the Word of God, and has brought to my remembrance what I needed to do in the service of the Lord. He has also kept me in serious times when the flesh would have responded differently.

How can one be saved?

By confessing that one is a sinner then believing in one's heart and receiving Christ into one's life. (*Romans* 10:9–10 *and John* 1:12).

Brother Jon Dyer

Background:

My name is Jon Dyer. I was born on June 12, 1971 in Worcester, MA to Wilbur and Eunice Dyer, both of whom believed in giving me a good education which coincidently was the biggest influence in my spiritual life. As a young man, all of my elementary education was in a Catholic school. I was also a member of a catholic all boys choir, where I felt a profound call to ministry. My father was the first black union electrician in Worcester, MA and directed me into that vocation. By the time I was 26-years old and finding success in my work, I was approached by a fellow tradesman and through several conversations was asked, "If you died right now where would you go?" All my money, friends, and status could not fill the emptiness I felt. As a result of that question, I started to attend a Baptist church. I then gave myself wholly to every gathering, prayer, Bible study, choir practice, youth group, and service not knowing that all the tradition or religion in the world could not replace the truth I was not receiving. In the summer of 1998, I received the Holy Ghost without knowing what had happened to me. About 2 years later, I met brother Stephen Cimini of an Apostolic Church, who told me what it truly meant to be saved (*Acts* 2:38). Not long after that, I was re-baptized in Jesus's name and was filled all over again. In 2002, led by Elder Kurt Geddis, a Bible study started in my living room and the rest is history. *Thank you for witnessing to me, Brother Dyer. You truly saved my life through Christ.*

Who do you consider a born-again Christian?

Anyone who has received the Holy Ghost evidenced by speaking in other tongues, have been baptized in Jesus's name and believes the gospel of Jesus Christ.

What does eternal life mean to you?

The intensity of the joy, euphoria, peace, love, and power of receiving the Holy Ghost forever in the present tense.

What is your experience with the Holy Ghost?

Through God's Spirit I have experienced the comfort of a friend, the encouragement of a father, the defense of a lawyer, and the healing of a great physician.

How can one be saved?

One must first acknowledge what one knows to be sin and become godly sorrowful about sinning. One must then confess one's sin to God and to the man of God, become willing to turn from sin, and acknowledge that the only cleansing from sin comes from being baptized in Jesus's name. One has to then open one's life to the leading of God away from a sinful lifestyle unto a holy one and then the Holy Ghost will be received. One is then saved.

Antenique Chambers

Background:

I am 27-years old. Church has and always will be constant in my life. I don't remember a time when I ever wasn't in church. I am Pastor Chambers's daughter. Thus, I am a preacher's kid, also known as a PK, and I think my life was a little different as a result of being one. My dad has been a minister all of my life and later became a pastor when I was around 9-years old. My mother is a Sunday school teacher. As a result, I attended church every Sunday, as well as Sunday school and Vacation Bible School. The type of church I attended was a Baptist church. There was Sunday morning service, afternoon service sometimes, Wednesday night prayer and Bible study, and sometimes a weekend activity. There was Vacation Bible School every year for either 1–2 weeks in the summer. I have always enjoyed being in church. I have always had an eagerness to learn more about God's Word. I was always the child in Sunday school who had actually studied the lesson prior to arriving to church, took notes on the minister's sermon, and who knew her Bible well when it came time to finding scriptures.

Who do you consider a born-again Christian?

My perception of a born-again Christian is someone who has repented and wants to turn his life around and strive to be more like Christ each and everyday.

What does eternal life mean to you?

Eternal life is a life where I don't have to focus on the problems and stresses of the world, but a life where Jesus is the focus and there is nothing to interfere with that.

What is your experience with the Holy Ghost?

I tend to get very emotional when I am filled with the Holy Ghost. I am just so overwhelmed and thankful when I think of God's blessings that a flood of emotions come over me and I give praise to God.

How can one be saved?

In order to become saved, one must confess his sins (repent) and believe that the Lord Jesus Christ was dead, buried, and rose again. The individual must also desire to have a personal relationship with Jesus Christ. After this the individual is then baptized in order to witness to others their acceptance of Jesus Christ into their life.

Sister Jessica Rodriguez

Background:

I am a 24-year-old Hispanic-American female of the Apostolic faith. I am Brother Bailey's sister in Christ, of the New Hope Apostolic Church in Worcester, Massachusetts. My parents are from Puerto Rico. They came to this land in the mid-60's. They stayed married through good weather and bad storms. I was born and raised in the harsh city of Boston, Massachusetts, where many have strayed away. I am a single mother of one. His name is Matthew. In this land of America, many fail to acknowledge Jesus, the God of heaven, who came to die for the sins of this world. I strongly believe in the Word of God and attend a God-fearing church; where we strongly believe that it is important for the saints of God to befriend, fellowship with, and encourage each other.

Who do you consider a born-again Christian?

I consider one to be a born-again Christian when one has obeyed the commands of Christ in order to be saved. One who has turned from one's evil ways and has been born again of the water and of the fire by the Holy Ghost (*John 3:5*). One is a Christian when one is trying to be like Christ according to the Word of God.

What does eternal life mean to you?

Eternal life is one dying and entering into a new existence, where there will be no more tears, no more death, no more wars, or battles to stand against. Existing where the beauty of God is ever surrounding in a place where peace abounds throughout a land that shall never pass away.

What is your experience with the Holy Ghost?

This experience is like none other. The Holy Ghost has been to me as though I were a crystal cup and a fountain so pure pouring itself into my cup as it overflowed with joy. The Holy Ghost has also been to me like a dry desert place longing for a drop of rain and the floodgates of heaven opening and quenched my thirst. My Holy Ghost experience is more than my thrill of riding a horse or going unicorn white water rafting up north. Jesus, my Lord and savior redeemed my soul and freed me from the chains of this world.

How can one be saved?

One may be saved by sincerely repenting of one's sins and turn from one's evil ways and lifestyle that is not like God. One must then be immersed in the water being baptized in one name alone, being Jesus (*Matthew* 1:21) and receiving the gift of the Holy Ghost (*Acts* 2:38) with the evidence of speaking with other tongues. Finally, one must continue on the course with Jesus, striving to live Holy and as a living witness of Christ. Behold the power and Glory of Jesus!

Andrea Johnson

Background:

I am An African-American female raised in the Presbyterian Church. I attended Christian and Catholic schools until 7th grade. While I was christened at the church in which I grew up, I was baptized as an adult, as my mother believed that your baptism was a personal choice. I primarily attended Presbyterian churches until my mid-30's at which time I started attending a non-denominational church. Zion Church, in Largo, Maryland is more of a teaching church that allows its members to come as they are, hear the Word, and gain a better understanding of spirituality, Christianity, and living a Christ-filled life.

Who do you consider a born-again Christian?

I consider anyone who has found a faith and has a solid belief in the Lord after having spent time not focused on faith or spirituality, a born-again Christian. I think that many people as they traverse life lose their way and are internally redirected to God and spirituality.

What does eternal life mean to you?

Eternal life means that when your physical body dies your spirit continues to live on according to your spiritual belief system. I believe that you are finally at a place in which you reach a truly peaceful spiritual existence.

What is your experience with the Holy Ghost?

My experience with the Holy Ghost/Spirit is that the Holy Spirit is what guides you through life and leads you to make the right decisions. The Holy Spirit is your intuition and that small voice that guides you through life and attempts to help you to become the best person physically and spiritually.

How can one be saved?

Being saved is a Christian tenet that is defined as someone who believes in God and Jesus Christ and that accepts Jesus as one's personal Lord and Savior.

Elder Kurt W. Geddis

Background:

I am from Hartford, Connecticut. I have been around the Apostolic faith/church all my life, which was a second home for me. At the age of thirteen, March 13, 1977 Jesus truly came into my life and filled me with the precious gift of the Holy Ghost, with the evidence of speaking with other tongues as the Spirit of God gave me utterance. I have not looked back since. I am an African-American male Apostolic preacher of the New Hope Apostolic Church in Massachusetts. I am now 44-years old. I have been a minister for 20 years and have been pastoring for 6 years.

Who do you consider a born-again Christian?
Those who obey *John* 3:5.

What does eternal life mean to you?
Being with Jesus forever and away from the people.

What is your experience with the Holy Ghost?
The Holy Ghost leads me, teaches me, guides me, strengthens me, and gives me discernment.

How can one be saved?
One can be saved by repenting of one's sins, baptizing in Jesus's name, and by receiving the gift of the Holy Ghost (*Acts* 2:38) with the evidence of speaking with other tongues as the Spirit of God gives utterance (*Acts* 2:4).

Fr. James Mazzone,
Diocese of Worcester, MA

Background:
He is the priest/director of vocations at the Holy Name of Jesus Parish in Massachusetts. He

grew up in the town of Spencer, Massachusetts, where he went to public schools from kindergarten to grade 12. He then went on to obtain his Bachelors of Arts in Theology at Saint Anselm College in New Hampshire. After college, he had seven more years of education to be the priest that he is today. He is 39-years old. In 2001, he was a ground zero chaplain in New York City after the world trade center bombing. He has been a priest since 1999 and has ministered in seven countries, including France, Italy, South Africa, and Egypt.

Who do you consider a born-again Christian?

Well, born-again Christian is not a common term of the Catholic faith. The faith is a journey; it is a lifelong process with certain channels of grace, which comes through sacraments. The sacraments as a whole are seen as a necessary means of salvation for the faithful. The sacraments were instituted by Christ to the Church. These include baptism, Eucharist, and confirmation.

What does eternal life mean to you?

Eternal life is seeing God face to face for eternity. No more pain or sorrow. Just being in perfect peace.

What is your experience with the Holy Ghost?

Since one in the Catholic faith is baptized as a young child, one needs to go through confirmation to receive the Holy Spirit. During confirmation you are asked if you want to continue on the faith. After confirming to continue on the faith, you are then sealed with the Holy Spirit by the priest anointing your forehead with oil. The Holy Spirit is what Jesus left behind. It empowers us. We should pray that it remains in and works in us. It gives us an extra power through trials. It gives me an extra boost of energy when I should be tired. Sometimes, I find myself saying, "I am on Holy Spirit power."

How can one be saved?

This is a tough one. One is saved by God's grace and mercy. One should live a good moral life, be a giver, and love others. One should fall in love with Jesus. God's grace and mercy is what saves and gets us to heaven.

LeeRoy Bailey, Jr.
(Author of This Book)

Email address: brnagain@gmail.com *(Please email only if you truly want to be saved)*

Who do you consider a born-again Christian?

One who is baptized in Jesus's name and has received the gift of the Holy Ghost.

What does eternal life mean to you?

Living forever with Jesus in paradise when this old world passes away. Goodbye world.

What is your experience with the Holy Ghost?

The Holy Ghost quickens my mortal body and shakes me all over; as if I have veins loaded with electricity. I speak with other tongues as the Spirit of God gives me utterance and I have the power to resist the temptations of the devil. I also hear myself groaning sometimes when I pray, which means the Holy Ghost is praying on my behalf just like the Bible reads.

How can one be saved?

According to the scriptures, being a born-again Christian and how one can be saved are interchangeable. You cannot be a born-again Christian if you are not saved and you are not saved if you have not been born again. Being saved, you have the pass to eternal life. Being saved also requires you to have the Holy Ghost and be baptized in Jesus's name. Thus, in order to be saved; you must be born again.

On one hand, in *John* 3:5, Jesus responds to how one can be born again. On the other hand, in *Acts* 2:38, Peter responds to how one can be saved. Both responses include being baptized and receiving the Holy Ghost. Believe me not? Read the above scriptures and ask God to open your eyes. It is truly plain and simple. The latter scriptures also include Jesus. In one scripture Jesus tells us that we need to be born again/saved. The other reads about being baptized in the name of Jesus Christ in order for you to have your sins washed away and to be saved. My friends, if you are not born again in Jesus, you cannot enter into heaven, neither will you have eternal life. Thus, you have not been saved from this wicked world. People have many different answers to the four vital questions asked in this chapter, but Jesus is the only way to heaven (*John* 14:6). This is what I believe according to the Holy Scriptures. My brethren, I do not know what heaven is like, but the Bible says it is paradise (*Revelation* 2:7). If there is anything I know about paradise, is that it is a happy place. All you need is there. Like the gospel duo, Mary Mary sang, "I gotta get myself together, cause I got someplace to go. And I'm praying when I get there, I see everyone I know. I wanna go to heaven, I wanna go … " Friends, I must reach heaven (*Isaiah* 65:17–25).

7.

God's Will for You

As it is written, it is not in the will of God, " ... that any should perish, but to come to repentance" (*2nd Peter* 3:9). In addition, God also said, "I have set before you, life, death, blessing, and cursing. Thus, choose life" (*Deuteronomy* 30:19). Friends, God is love. He loves us so very much. Do you love Him? Are you sure? Have you tried running away from yourself but there is no way of escape? Have all doors sometimes seem to be closed and not even a friend in sight in time of need? Is there no one to help you lately? Now is the time, my friend. Do not give up. Look to Jesus. There is hope. You just need faith. Believe it. There is a purpose for your life. Have faith, for the Lord said, " ... Many be called, but few are chosen" (*Matthew* 20:16). Do you want to be one of the chosen few? My friends, we are not as good as we think we are. Yes, you may go to church, but that does not mean all is well. You must repent of your sins. We are all sinners and unworthy creatures. We all need to be helped by God. There is truly nothing wrong with admitting that you are a sinner. This simply means that you have some integrity and are concerned about what is going on in your life. God is rich in mercy, which endures forever (*Ephesians* 2:4 and *Psalm* 136:1). Talk with Him. "Draw [close] to God, and He will draw [close] unto you. Cleanse your hands, ye sinners; and purify your hearts, ye double minded" (*James* 4:8). Return unto Him and He will return unto you (*Malachi* 3:7). Also my friends, a part of you coming to God includes paying your tithes. This is not a joke. A tenth of your paycheck belongs to the church (*Leviticus* 27:32 *and Genesis* 28:22). God will bless you for it (*Malachi* 3:10). The church acquires bills. This burden cannot be left on the pastor alone. Your tithes and offerings are your obligations to God. They should be the most important of all your bills.

Above all, let God purge you with His precious blood. In the name of Jesus, be baptized. "Lord, as I look at my life today, I realize that there are many things that are not like you. Lord, I repent, flush me Lord, flush me out. For I want to truly be in your perfect and divine will." My God, my God, "Why do the heathen rage and the people imagine a vain thing" (*Psalm* 2:1)? People, you need the Lord. When will we comprehend that we must give our lives to Him? You could put on your wings in the morning and try to fly away, but there is no escape from God (*Psalm* 139:9-10). You better hear me, repent, for you need the Lord. Jesus is the Way, the Truth, and the Life. No one goeth to the Father in heaven but by Him. If you open up your ears, heart, and mind God will reveal Himself to you. Accept a true man of God into your life, a genuine pastor that will open up the unadulterated Word of the Lord to you. A pastor that will show you love, warmth, guidance, kindness, and care. One who will be there for you and will present to you the plan of salvation. Now, contrary to popular belief, you do not get to choose your own pastors. God gave us pastors after His own heart (*Jeremiah* 3:15). Thus, the next time someone invites you to church, assess the situation and make sure that you are in a church of sound doctrine. For it just might be the Lord reaching out to you.

We all need sound doctrine and a true man of God to guide us. The Ethiopian eunuch in the desert told Phillip that he could not understand the Word of God unless someone guides him (*Acts* 8:31). Anyhow, with all that has been written, not every pastor is a true pastor. No one can truly preach, unless he is sent by God (*Romans* 10:15). Thus, accept a pastor that is real. Ask God to guide you. You will know a pastor by his fruits. Evil cannot come from good (*Matthew* 12:35). So, if he is a true pastor, it will show in his church members and in his works for the Lord. Be wise! God also gave us common sense. You know who and what is right from wrong because it is in the Word. Lastly, after receiving a true pastor and church from God, "Obey them that have the rule over you, and submit yourselves: for they watch for your souls, as they that must give account, that they may do it with joy, and not with grief: for that is unprofitable for you" (*Hebrews* 13:17). Be wise, you must obey the men of God. If they steer you wrong, God will take care of it (*Jeremiah* 23:1). You just do your part by being obedient to the Word that comes from the men of God.

Backsliders, you who know the truth, but decided to walk according to the course of this world, according to the prince (devil) of the power of the air, who is the spirit that now works in [you], the children of disobedience (*Ephesians* 2:2), please come back to your Father, which is Jesus. There is no hope without Him. Hear me please. As for you who are saved, and staying on the path of righteousness, please do not go back to the beggarly elements of sin (*Galatians* 4:9). Do not do this to yourselves, you may never return of your own accord. For by grace are ye saved through faith; and that not of yourselves: It is the gift of God (*Ephesians* 2:8). If you commit a sin against God, do not throw in the towel. Do not let the devil tell you that you cannot come back to Jesus. Repent I say and come back, lest ye die and your soul abides in hell (*Luke* 13:3). Saved folks, stay saved! Keep your head in the Bible. The Word will be " … a lamp unto [your] feet and a light unto [your] path" (*Psalm* 119:105). The Word of God will guide you unto glory. Backsliders, again I urge you, make haste and come back. God takes no pleasure in you (*Hebrews* 10:38), nor are you fit for the kingdom of God (*Luke* 9:62). You know truth, abide therein, lest ye die in your sin and your righteousness shall not be remembered (*Ezekiel* 3:20). Saints, God is not playing with us. If you take fire in your bosom, you will get burned (*Proverbs* 6:27). Do not play with fire or sin. God gave us a chance through His grace and mercy. We are called to witness of His honor and glory, not to be unholy. Please, do not be lukewarm for Christ (*Revelation* 3:16) and take Him for granted, He will spew you out, lay a stumbling block before you, and take your life (*Ezekiel* 3:20)!

Again, I will ask you two very important questions: What if you live for the Lord, get baptized in Jesus's name like Peter said in *Acts* 2:38, get filled with the Holy Ghost, and remain true to the Word of God, but then found out Jesus is not real? Well, you could just continue living. No harm in that. But, what if you live a lying, fornicating, stealing, partying, killing, adulterous, prideful, lustful, anyone of the above sinful life, then come to find out that Jesus is real as I know He is and that His every word is true, what will you do then? Again I say, I do not know about you, but I refuse to find out the hard way. Remember, it is only by the blood of the lamb and our testimonies of Jesus Christ that we will overcome the devil (*Revelation* 12:11). We, that are truly Holy Ghost-filled are more than conquerors and nothing, life, death, angels, principalities, things present, nor things to come, height, depth, nor any other creature shall be able to separate us from the love of God, which is in Jesus Christ our Lord (*Romans* 8:37–39). We have the quickening power to withstand the wiles of the devil through Jesus.

Friend, this is where I end and God will do the rest. "Call unto me, and I will answer thee, and shew thee great and mighty things, which thou knowest not" (*Jeremiah* 33:3). My words have I put in thy mouth (*Jeremiah* 1:9). The Lord will speak through you if you let Him. Salvation, my friend, is free. Any day you ask Jesus to come into your life, He will never turn from you (*Hebrews* 13:5). So, please, make that any day, today. This is the chapter where you reflect on Jesus. I am finished. I planted a seed in you through Him. He will now water that seed and increase your faith through your reflections on

Him (1*st Corinthians* 3:7). You know what you want, but you do not know what He wants for you. Do not wait until you are old to come to Christ. Please, remember your Creator in the days of your youth before the difficult days come (*Ecclesiastes* 12:1). Do not wait too long. You may grow wax cold. Seek Christ now!

Please, listen to the Word of God. For when anyone hears the Word of God, and does not understand it, then the evil one comes and takes away that which was sown in one's heart. This is one, who has received seed by the way side (*Matthew* 13:19). Ask Jesus to reveal His will for you to you. Grow spiritually in Him and He will guide your path. Most importantly, love Him. For " ... eye hath not seen, nor ear heard, neither have entered into the heart of man, the things which God hath prepared for them that love Him" (1*st Corinthians* 2:9). God is able to do exceeding abundantly above all things that we ask or think (*Ephesians* 3:20). Ask in prayer for what you need of Him. He loves us.

Your job now is to reflect and write down whatever it is that Jesus is speaking to your heart at this moment. This is your opportunity to hear from God. Listen to Him! My friend, listen and follow through with all He is putting in your heart right now, as you become pensive. For now is the accepted time to be saved (2*nd Corinthians* 6:2). God bless you and thank you for reading. May peace also be multiplied unto you. The grace of our Lord, Jesus

Christ of Nazareth be with you all, in Jesus's name I pray, Amen.

Jesus said, "… One thing thou lackest: go thy way, sell whatever thou hast, and give to the poor, and thou shalt have treasure in heaven: and come, take up the cross, and follow me" (*Mark* 10:21). "… Holy, holy, holy, is the Lord of hosts: the whole earth is full of His glory" (*Isaiah* 6:3). Be ye holy, like your Father in heaven is holy (1*st Peter* 1:16).

"Not every one that saith unto me, Lord, Lord, shall enter into the kingdom of heaven; but he that doeth the will of my Father which is in heaven" (Mathew 7:21).

" ... *Without ceasing I have remembrance of thee in my prayers night and day; greatly desiring to see thee, being mindful of thy tears, that I may be filled with joy*" (*2nd Timothy* 1:3–4).

Reflections and writing:

Reflections and writing:

Reflections and writing:

Emergency Phone Numbers:

When in sorrow,...................................call John 14.
When men fail you,..............................call Psalm 27.
When you have sinned,........................call Psalm 51.
When you are in danger,.......................call Psalm 91.
When God seems far away,..................call Psalm 139.
When your faith needs stirring,.........call Hebrews 11.
When you are lonely and fearful,...........call Psalm 23.
When you feel down and out,........call Romans 8:31.
When you grow bitter and critical,...........................
....call 1 Corinthians 13.
When you worry,...................call Matthew 6:19–34.
When you want peace and rest,.............................
....call Matthew 11:25–30.
When you want Christian assurance,......................
....call Romans 8:1–30.
When you think of investments and returns,..........
....call Malachi 3:10.
When the world seems bigger than God,...................
....call Psalm 90.
When you leave home for labor and travel,...............
....call Psalm 121.

When your prayers grow narrow or selfish,..............
....call Psalm 67.
When you want courage for a task,........call Joshua 1.
For a great invention/opportunity,........call Isaiah 55.
For how to get along with fellow men,.....................
....call Romans 12.
For Paul's secret to happiness,................................
....call Colossians 3:12–17.
For understanding of Christianity,...........................
....call 2 Corinthians 5:15–19.
*If you want to know about the oneness of God,........
.........call John 1:1–14, 1 John 5:7, 1 Timothy 3:16.
*If you want to know how to be prepared for heaven,
....call John 3:5–7.
*If you want to be born again of water and of the
Spirit (being saved),..............................call *Acts* 2:38.
*If you want to know the value of baptism in Jesus's
name,..........................call Romans 6, *Galatians* 3:27.
If you are losing confidence in people,............................
....call 1 Corinthians 13.
If discouraged about your work,........call Psalm 126.
If you are depressed,.............................call Psalm 27.
If your pocketbook is empty,................call Psalm 37.
If you find yourself great and the world small,.........
....call Psalm 19.
If people seem unkind,...........................call John 15.
If you want to be fruitful,.......................call John 15.

Alternate numbers:

For dealing with fear,..........................call Psalm 34:7.

For assurance,...................................call Mark 8: 35.

For security,.....................................call Psalm 121:3.

For reassurance,...............................call Psalm 145:18.

- *Emergency numbers may be dialed directly. No operator assistance is necessary.*
- *All lines to heaven are open 24 hours a day! Feed your faith, and doubt will start to die!*

-Anonymous and LeeRoy U. Bailey, Jr.